GUITAR MAN

GUITAR MAN

SIX STRINGS OF SEPARATION

M. J. INDELICATO

WITHDRAWN

HAL LEONARD BOOKS

An Imprint of Hal Leonard Corporation

Published in 2015 by Hal Leonard Books
An Imprint of Hal Leonard Corporation
7777 West Bluemound Road
Milwaukee, WI 53213

Trade Book Division Editorial Offices
33 Plymouth St., Montclair, NJ 07042

Printed in the United States of America

Book design by Michael Kellner

Library of Congress Cataloging-in-Publication Data
Indelicato, M. J., author.
 Guitar man : six strings of separation / M.J. Indelicato.
    pages cm
 Includes index.
 ISBN 978-1-4950-2655-3
 1. Guitar--Collectors and collecting. I. Title.
 ML1015.G9I58 2015
 787.87'19075--dc23
                                2015029971
www.halleonardbooks.com

"My Car Is My Castle"

I have a house but it ain't no home
Got a car but I'm all alone
Have some cash
Got a phone
Through the States
Therefore I roam

—MICHAEL INDELICATO

Contents

Prologue

I t's often a happy but bumpy landing at McCarran Airport in Las Vegas. The hot air of the desert floor combines with the cooler temperatures of the surrounding mountains to create a phenomenon known as "wind shear." This condition makes it downright tricky to land a big ol' jet airliner in Vegas, and this flight was to be no exception. As we got close to the runway, the 737 was thrown around like a boy on a bucking bronco: up 50 feet one second, down 150 yards a moment later.

Predictably, our captain announced: "Ladies and gentlemen, we're experiencing some slight turbulence. Please keep your seat belts fastened and remain in your seats until the safety belt sign has been turned off."

The impeccably dressed woman reading a magazine in the seat next to me seemed rather blasé about the "slight" turbulence on our approach.

"Weekend of gambling?" she inquired, peering over her massive Prada sunglasses.

"Something like that," was my uneasy reply.

It was rather odd that this woman had waited to the end of the flight to engage me in conversation, and even more peculiar that she did so just after the plane lurched and the passengers let out a collective groan. If it wasn't yet obvious that I was scared half to death, it was so by the time the formerly cheery, syrupy-sweet-voiced flight attendant chimed in on the intercom attempting to calm us.

"Just a little bumpy," she said. "Not to worry . . . we'll have you on the ground in just a few minutes."

And then, without a trace of fear in her voice, the attendant deadpanned: "Welcome to McCarran, Las Vegas."

Isn't it just a wee bit curious when they "welcome" you to an airport before you have even landed? Especially on a day like this one, when it seems more likely than not that the plane is going down like a lead zeppelin.

The passenger to my right, still calmly engaged in reading her *Horse and Hound* magazine, was correct. I had come to Las Vegas to gamble—but it was not at a slot machine, nor in front of a blackjack table, nor even with a pack of hungry hyenas at a craps table. No, there was nothing dicey about what I was placing my bet on. It was a guitar—a 1959 Rickenbacker electric guitar, to be exact. You see, earning the title "vintage guitar dealer" requires that I travel all across this great land of ours to find them. These old guitars can be surprisingly valuable and extremely coveted. Even though I have owned thousands of vintage guitars, today's trip was special, for I had stumbled onto a guitar that was supremely rare and remarkably valuable: it was a Rickenbacker guitar virtually identical to the one that John Lennon had played in his early days as a Beatle.

Rickenbacker, a venerable California guitar company, first started making guitars in 1927. They not only manufactured the world's first electric guitar in 1931, but thirty-one years later produced the guitar that Lennon performed with on the *Ed Sullivan Show* on February 9, 1964. Lennon's guitar was known as the Rickenbacker 325 model. The instrument I was coming to purchase was one of only five of these 325 model Rickenbackers made in 1959—and it was only a few serial numbers away from Mr. Lennon's guitar. That alone made it a treasure. That the guitar was in mint condition, and that the seller even had the original paperwork with this rare bird, made it a collector's dream guitar. But what made it even more thrilling and relevant to me was that the guitar was manufactured the same week I was born. It seemed to me that the stars were indeed lined up for me to own this gem.

I planned to add this guitar to my private collection as a "keeper" (as we aficionados call them). However, first things first—I had to get to Las Vegas in one piece. The only thing standing between that Rickenbacker and me was a safe landing by our good pilot, Captain Merrill Winthrop.

Even as Captain Winthrop lined up the Las Vegas landing strip from miles back, it was apparent that he was having difficulty keeping the aircraft on a straight trajectory. Yet as we descended from an altitude of one thousand feet, to seven hundred feet, followed by five hundred feet, it seemed as if we were going to make a safe landing after all. But at three hundred feet a large gust of wind hit the plane so hard that it almost tilted the right wing into the ground. As the plane pitched and rolled violently back, El Capitan hit the throttle hard—so hard, in fact, we went nearly vertical. Yikes!

After twenty choppy minutes of circling the airport, we finally got the all clear to land—and this time made a hard but decisive touchdown. As I departed the aircraft, I asked the visibly shaken flight attendant if this was a regular occurrence.

"No," she said, out of breath, flashing me a strained, laser-whitened smile. "Sometimes we circle in a holding pattern when the weather is rough, but getting that close to the ground and then aborting the landing? Never. First time in twenty years of flying."

"Really?" I replied. "This is my second white-knuckle landing in the past six months."

It was.

As I walked away, the attendant looked at me like I was a miracle survivor boy or something. And in a way she was correct; in some perverse manner of the universe, this episode seemed like a telling metaphor for my life as a guitar hunter. On the one hand, there have been a great number of smooth sailings and many happy landings in my travels in search of these old guitars. Along this pathway I have bought and sold thousands of instruments and made *mucho dinero*. Yet, on the other hand, like my trip to Vegas, there have been the troubled passages, fraught with danger and near disaster. However, all in all, I've always somehow managed to land with my feet planted on terra firma.

And yes, it did seem as if the guitar gods were smiling down on me that sunny, windswept afternoon. Yet by the time I arrived in Vegas, the nice man with the Rickenbacker 325 had changed his mind about selling me his guitar. I went home empty-handed.

Just like they say in the casinos . . . better luck next time, chump.

1

SETTING THE TONE

It was in the early spring of 1975, March 14 to be exact, that, with a ticket clenched in my sweaty fist, I entered the legendary portals of Winterland Arena in San Francisco. I have since marked the date as my first true rock concert. I had previously seen Elton John perform at the Oakland Coliseum; and he put on a superb show, but I always counted him as more of a pop performer.

There was nothing "pop" about Winterland; it was one of the last vestiges of classic sixties San Francisco *rock* culture. In 1971, it replaced the iconic Fillmore West just across Geary Boulevard as pioneering concert promoter Bill Graham's preeminent venue in the Bay Area. Winterland had no less an impact on musical history than its decidedly smaller predecessor. At Winterland, Graham showcased such superstar bands as the Rolling Stones, Led Zeppelin, the Who, the Jimi Hendrix Experience, Janis Joplin, Santana, Cream, and scores of others.

The Winterland Arena started out as a boxing hall in 1928, and then became an ice skating rink before it was leased by Graham as a concert venue. The grand old wooden structure had naturally good acoustics that could make just about anyone sound great—not that the names playing there needed help. Winterland was considered home to the Grateful Dead, who would play there almost sixty times over the course of their career. It was also the setting for *The Last Waltz*, a documentary directed by Martin Scorsese chronicling the farewell performance of the Band, with special guests Bob Dylan, Neil Young, Eric Clapton, Van Morrison, and Muddy Waters, to name a few. Peter Frampton cut *Frampton Comes Alive!* there in 1975, which went on to become the top-selling live album in history. On December 15–16, 1978, Bruce Springsteen recorded a Winterland concert that is considered by historians to be one of the Boss's most legendary shows. A lot of famous feet walked those hallowed, sound-seasoned boards in that old building located at the corner of Post and Steiner.

On that misty March night in '75 my brother and I, along with two friends, joined a sea of young fans that had come in search of a little Winterland magic. An interesting side note says something about the tenor of the times: those two teenage friends had been arrested for holding up a grocery store at gunpoint several weeks before. The store owner had even taken a couple of pot shots at the boys as they tried to make their getaway! The youthful banditos were quickly apprehended, but just as quickly released on probation—just in time to join us on our pilgrimage to Winterland. There was still a bit of the Wild West that lingered in that time and place, or at least in the scrappy blue-collar neighborhood where I grew up. It was, in many ways, a more innocent age. The parents of the two delinquents had to escort them to the show as a condition of probation, which is also the only reason I got to go in the first place. None of us had a car or was licensed to drive.

As we handed over our tickets and walked through the wide double doors into the teeming lobby, a man with a hooded sweatshirt and dark, piercing eyes greeted us with a clammy handshake. We didn't realize that this was the era's premier rock concert promoter himself: Bill Graham. Of course, at that age I had no idea who Bill Graham might be. I just assumed patrons were greeted with a personal welcome at every show.

Graham's success had less to do with making customers feel comfortable than with packing venues to the rafters. In typical fashion, this concert was sold out and then some. Graham had an eccentric habit of selling extra tickets for every show. We were packed in, elbow-to-elbow, cheek-to-jowl, and just about every other body part you might care to mention. Since we were still in the midst of the great countercultural youth revolution, there were a lot of nubile women in attendance decked out in hippie-rock regalia, with short-cut tie-dye shirts, tight-fitting bell-bottom jeans, and platform shoes, which made being in such close proximity considerably more tolerable.

It was a night of many firsts for me. One fetching young girl in a headband actually reached through the forest of arms and legs to grope me. "You like that?" she asked. I was too tongue-tied to reply with the obvious answer. As in many moments of unique personal significance—you had to be there. Beach balls were batted over the top of the dense crowd, cheers erupting as they bounced across the sparkling expanse. The pungent smell of cannabis smoke swirled, though since that particular odor was new to me, my friends had to explain to me what it was. But there was no mistaking the smell of spilled beer and the sawdust that had been spread liberally across the concrete floor to sop it up. Yes, the beer was flowing, the marijuana was thick in the air and the place was packed with gorgeous girls. I felt like a fledgling bird that had been pushed out of the nest for the first time. I was seeing a whole new world and I knew instinctively that I was meant to be a part of it.

Having been born and raised not far from Winterland in the fabled San Francisco Bay Area, I was a child of the suburbs, and attuned early on to the great musical traditions that grew in and around those beautiful environs. Even before the world-famous sixties consciousness revolution, San Francisco had a reputation for innovation and individuality. I have always felt myself fortunate to be a witness to that freedom of expression, and to the great jazz, R&B, pop, and of course rock 'n' roll sounds that echoed off its steep streets.

My own family had an abiding love for music, dating back to my grandfather, Bill Scoggins. "Grandpa Bill" was, for a short time, the fiddle player in the most famous western swing band of all time—Bob Wills and the Texas Playboys. Gramps passed on to me a love of American roots music, and along the way I picked up some of his musical proclivities. For one thing, he was adept at a lot of instruments, including the fiddle, banjo, and piano. I always assumed that my appreciation of finely crafted musical tools came, at least in part, from him. The odd thing was that no one else in the family ever played an instrument. I was the first since my grandfather to show early interest in playing music, not simply keeping up with the Top 40 on the radio or going to the many clubs and concerts featuring local bands.

Like many contemporaries, one of my earliest musical memories is hearing the Beatles for the first time. It was 1964 and I was not yet five years old when the Beatles debuted on the *Ed Sullivan Show* on February 9. Shortly thereafter, my mother came home with *Meet the Beatles*, the Fab Four's debut album. Not long after that an uncle presented me with a set of classic Beatle bobblehead dolls. I still have them to this day (and no way, they're not for sale).

Just a scant two and a half years after their debut on the *Ed Sullivan Show*, the Beatles played the last concert of their U.S.

tour at Candlestick Park in San Francisco. As it turns out, it was to be their last public concert *ever*. This August 29, 1966, farewell was an unmistakable sign that the musical center of gravity had shifted from England to the California coast. During those tremendously exciting years, San Francisco and the Bay Area became the hub of the musical universe: the Grateful Dead, Creedence Clearwater Revival, Santana, the Jefferson Airplane, Janis Joplin—all called San Francisco "home." Music truly was everywhere, including my own home, where my parents constantly had influential vinyl spinning on the turntable.

And by the time I was ten years old, I was the proud owner of my own source of music: a portable radio. I spent countless hours on the back deck of our home, staring up at the stars, listening with rapt attention to KFRC-AM. The richness and variety of the music and the talent that produced it was unprecedented. It was the late sixties, a phenomenal time to be alive and the heyday of classic American and English popular music.

The music reached beyond the airwaves; it was a force for personal transformation, shaping and inspiring lives, including mine. I will never forget one special moment of illumination. The year was 1974 and I was at a friend's house watching *Don Kirshner's Rock Concert*, the premier television show for new and established acts. One of the featured attractions that evening was The Edgar Winter Group playing the massive instrumental hit "Frankenstein." The guitarist featured on the TV show was one Mr. Rick Derringer. For someone who already had a love for music, seeing Derringer play the guitar was amazing.

My appreciation must have shown in my expression, because my friend's sister Jill sat next to me and said, "If you like this guy, you're going to love Robin Trower."

Robin who? I'd never even heard the name. I was vaguely familiar with the worldwide hit "A Whiter Shade of Pale," from the pioneering British band Procol Harum, but I never knew the group's lineup, much less that it featured a guitar maestro who had since gone on to form his own trio. Trower was a wizard of feedback-drenched tonality, with an incredibly distinctive vibrato technique. Once you hear him play, you can instantly recognize his trademarked sound. And it was an experience I was inspired to have forthwith.

The very next day, I mounted my bicycle and urgently pedaled the eight miles from my East Bay home in the small suburban community of El Sobrante to my destination: the A&L Record Store in San Pablo. A&L had the most extensive inventory of albums in the area. When I arrived on that warm spring afternoon I was disappointed to learn that the album Jill had recommended, *Bridge of Sighs*, was not in stock. They did, however, have a copy of Robin Trower's first release, *Twice Removed from Yesterday*.

I agonized long and hard that afternoon, asking myself whether I should invest the whole $5.49 or hold off and come back for the album Jill had recommended. Now, five and a half snaps was a lot of money in 1974. Was one record better than the other? Having never heard a note of Trower's music, I had no idea. But after I'd spent half an hour looking at the cover of *Twice Removed from Yesterday*, with its enchanting tones of rich blue depicting a mysterious spherical shape that seemed to be intersecting unknown dimensions of time and space, I said out loud, "This is beautiful artwork. Maybe that speaks to the music inside."

So I bought it, sped home, popped it on the turntable immediately, and comprehensively loved it. I listened to that album constantly. Later I would learn that Robin Trower's music had been compared to that of Jimi Hendrix. Even though Hendrix had passed just three and a half years earlier, and everyone in my high school was still talking about him, I did not know who

Mr. Hendrix was, nor was I familiar with his music at that time. Well, that was soon to change.

As one might have guessed, *Twice Removed from Yesterday* was a milestone in my musical journey. Not only was it the first album I ever purchased, but it turned out to be a stunning combination of songwriting, vocals, drumming, and guitar virtuosity that spoke in a rich and revealing new language. Since the album cover had no band photographs front or back, I did not know what the lineup of the group might be. I even wondered if Robin Trower might be a woman. I quizzed everyone I knew about clues to this elusive artist and his (or her) musical antecedents, but no one seemed to know more than that Trower had once been in Procol Harum and had gone on to form his (or her) own group featuring his own highly developed guitar style.

My next order of business was to hunt down Trower's second album, the elusive *Bridge of Sighs*. I eventually found it, and it was immediately apparent that this was one of the great albums of that era. Over time, I wore out the grooves on that record with constant playing. My interest in music was really getting started and the guitar was now the main fascination of it all. So when we entered Winterland to see Robin Trower and his band perform on that March evening in 1975, I was tremendously excited to see this fabled musician in action.

After spending some time taking in the aforementioned sights, sounds, and smells of this old concert hall, we eventually made our way high into the hazy balcony seats just as the recorded music faded along with the lights. Finally, the seething sea of humanity was plunged into darkness. It was show time. I will never forget the sixty-cycle hum and the piercing red lights of the Marshall guitar amplifiers that stood like a phalanx just behind the spot where Trower was about to stand. After a moment, Bill Graham, the impresario himself, took the stage and

I was astounded to recognize the man who had greeted us at the door. Green fog poured from a smoke machine, enveloping the stage with mist tinted precisely the same shade as the back cover of Trower's latest album. A radiant energy consumed the crowd as Graham appropriately announced with full vaudevillian inflection, "Out of the green London fog—Robin Trower!"

It was then that Trower himself stepped from the haze like a modern Moses parting a green sea. His guitar, a 1956 Stratocaster, flashed reflections of the eerie light. As he hit the opening chords of his first number, the place was transformed: it was one of his most moving anthems and a favorite song of mine, "Day of the Eagle." The song began simply enough, with a guitar chord reminiscent of an alarm clock ringing. Then Trower turned suddenly to a seven-note pattern on an open E string, followed by another chord that culminated in a heavenly vibrato. All this was sweetened by a James Brown–style R&B up-tempo riff that carried the song. It was one thing to listen to this music off the record, but it was quite another to be in the same room as the band played it live. The music was exhilarating, but it was those guitar notes—those beautiful notes—that made it seem as if I were hearing the very voice of God.

From that moment on, Trower could well have stepped into our midst straight off Mount Olympus. His band was impassioned, soulful . . . and loud. The singer and bass player, James Dewar, was one of the greats. Drummer and percussionist Bill Lordan had previously played with Sly and the Family Stone— and was amazing. However, it was the tone of that '56 Stratocaster guitar and those stacks of Marshall amps that really transfixed me. Simply put, Robin Trower and his band blew the roof off that rickety old icon of a joint that evening, and it was one man and his electric guitar that was at the center of all this divine action.

Years later, I still remember that night as a turning point in my yet young life. I crossed a line, from everything I had known to everything that was waiting for me. Perhaps it was even a transition point from adolescence to adulthood. Not surprisingly, my baptism of music at Winterland also cemented my determination to become a guitar player. "That's it," I told my brother, after the roar of the music died down, "I'm gettin' a guitar!" I knew right then that this was the art of my generation—and I did not want to miss the boat. It has been said that one great concert may not change the world, but it certainly did change mine.

2

SIX STRINGS OF SEPARATION

The guitar-playing bug had bitten me. Immediately after that Robin Trower concert, I bought a used guitar from a friend: a Fender Stratocaster. It was a beautiful black 1974 model—the very same model that Robin Trower played. But a transformative event happened a few months later when I opened up a copy of *Circus* magazine. Inside was an interview with none other than Mr. Trower himself. Trower discussed therein the virtues of the Fender Stratocaster guitar, but he added a caveat: he let it be known that he played an older Stratocaster almost exclusively—a 1956 model, to be exact. "The older Strats are head and shoulders over the new ones. What you are buying today amounts to an imitation of the real thing." *Excusez-moi?* Was Trower saying that my shiny new black Strat was an imitation? Well, then, I was going to have to go out there and find myself the "real deal," an older Stratocaster.

And, in a very strange turn of events, I walked into Primo Music, a small music store in Walnut Creek, California, just a few weeks after I read that fateful interview with Trower, and what did I spy hanging up on the wall but a beautiful 1955 Stratocaster, priced at $500. I quickly traded my 1974 Strat in on the 1950s model, and my father was kind enough to loan me the difference in cash so I could consummate the deal. When I took the guitar home and played it, it sounded divine. My 1955 Stratocaster looked and sounded almost exactly like Trower's 1956 Strat. And Mr. Trower was correct; you could just see and feel the superior craftsmanship of that old '55 Strat. Man, even the smell of that aged nitrocellulose lacquer was intoxicating. I was smitten. After I'd spent a few days with that guitar, I knew that these vintage instruments were going to be worth a fortune someday. The truth was that after the early 1960s the quality of American-made guitars had declined. By the mid-1970s that decline was unmistakable. Mr. Trower was correct; his 1956 Stratocaster was a much finer instrument than the same guitar made by the same company just twenty years later. The craftsmanship, and the quality of the materials used to make the guitars, had simply diminished.

So I told my father, who was a vintage car collector, of my new plan to start snapping up these old guitars. He said he would help me, and that is precisely what he did. Because of my pop's assistance I was able, by my nineteenth year, to amass a substantial vintage guitar collection. Sunburst Les Pauls, Broadcasters, Flying V's, Firebirds, custom color Stratocasters . . . I had them all. Then, after graduating high school, I worked a good job for several years and further parlayed my earnings into my vintage arsenal.

At that time, most vintage guitars were relatively cheap, I was making good money, and at every opportunity I turned a grocery store paycheck into yet another vintage instrument. My collection grew by leaps and bounds, as did the public's interest in these older fine fretted instruments. But my passion for collecting guitars was soon to be interrupted by my desire to receive a higher education. In short, I traded my pursuit of the next Stratocaster or Les Paul for a college degree.

I was starting college a few years later than most, but, like every other student, my studies took up the largest part of my time and the fairest portion of my finances. I vowed to return to guitar collecting after I had become a man of letters, or, as Shakespeare himself might have rightly described me after eight years of study—a bookish theoric.

My university studies had started in California before I relocated to the United Kingdom to attend graduate school. At one point I had to sell one of my most prized possessions: a 1959 Gibson Les Paul Standard that had previously belonged to acclaimed jazz fusion pioneer John McLaughlin. The proceeds from that Les Paul went to help pay tuition. That really stung. I also was forced to part with a number of other instruments that were not as significant, but nonetheless painful to let go.

When I made the move to Britain, I took a 1958 Les Paul Junior along on a whim. It probably was worth no more than $800 at the time—not too much of a loss if it should get damaged. Surprisingly, my fellow students were awed by that unassuming little guitar, which was quite a rarity on that side of the Atlantic.

"Crikey," one student marveled, "you've got an amazing vintage Gibson here." When I went to some of the vintage guitar stores in London, I discovered he was right. By British standards, my guitar was a real treasure.

Actually, the poor and paltry selection of American vintage guitars in England, and the sky-high asking prices, gave me the idea of spending the upcoming summer back in the States buying vintage instruments. I thought perhaps I could then sell these instruments to British collectors and players and double my money while still giving them a good deal.

When I finally completed my education, I realized I hadn't taken an actual vacation for over ten years. Needing some down time and a way to have a little fun, I couldn't think of a more diverting way to spend a summer than hunting down a few vintage specimens to help replenish my collection and perhaps make a buck or two.

At this time, the early nineties, another pursuit presented itself: the avocation of collecting authentic wooden duck decoys. What I learned from watching old pros buy and sell these often beautiful and historic hunting artifacts helped me tremendously in negotiating for guitars. Credit for my entry into the world of buying and selling—both guitars and decoys—is therefore due to a pair of skilled operators.

The first is my good friend Bill Mori, a successful real estate entrepreneur in Sonoma, California. For the past forty years, Bill has dedicated significant time to his first love, collecting old duck decoys, originally used by hunters to lure birds into shooting range. These decoys have become a prized and highly coveted form of folk art, especially those wooden decoys beautifully painted by skilled artisans before 1950.

Bill graciously took me under his wing and carefully taught me the fine art of evaluating and purchasing antique decoys. We would often spend an entire day visiting with people who were interested in selling decoys. Sometimes we traveled hundreds of miles to pursue a single lead. It was on such a trip that Bill first instilled in me the important principles of "working the living room." To become a successful buyer, he told me, there is nothing more important than establishing a rapport with the seller before you begin to discuss the item you hope to purchase. It was the approach I would later use to buy vintage guitars.

Many times I simply sat and listened as Bill chatted with decoy owners over the course of an afternoon. He would skillfully, but with sincere interest, get them to open up and share their life stories before he would even broach the notion of decoys and money changing hands. He was a natural buyer, with great intuition and polished people skills. Bill taught me that giving people a chance to tell their "story" was often the best way to let them know that you were not just interested in their decoys, but also in *them*. This in turn made it much more likely that they would sell their decoy(s) to you.

On one occasion, an older gentleman made a gift to Bill of ten valuable decoys, just because he appreciated Bill taking an hour to hear out some of the old man's duck hunting stories. Bill Mori is still widely known as the "decoy guru" by admiring collectors across the nation. The success I have enjoyed with vintage guitars is a direct result of his extended tutelage. The application of his timeless principle of the personal connection when meeting and greeting individuals from all walks of life has been invaluable.

The other good friend whose guidance, wisdom, and support proved critical in launching my guitar business was a man named Jack Ruggles. I first met Jack at the tender young age of fourteen when I dropped in to buy fishing tackle at his boating and sporting goods store, the United Boat Center in San Pablo, California. Jack's business was so successful that he was able to retire by the age of fifty-eight.

After selling his thriving boating and sports enterprise, Jack embarked on a new career as a decoy hustler. A gifted businessman with the common touch, he was nicknamed "Jackrabbit," and for good reason: no one could corner Jack Ruggles in a negotiation. He was always several hops ahead of the competition.

We hadn't seen each other in a number of years when, in 1985, I ran into Jack at a bustling summer flea market in Concord, California, where I was on my endless search for decoys and guitars. Thereafter, we rekindled our friendship.

No matter how valued a friend he was, nothing prepared me

for his singular act of generosity when I returned from my studies in England in 1991. Jack took me aside and, in his usual up-front and no-nonsense way, said, "Mike, you need to start making some money. I am going to loan you $50,000 so that you can get started in a business of your own." I was humbled by the faith and confidence he had in me, and that he was willing to back his belief with cash. However, this gracious offer was declined. Truth be told, no firm idea of a career had been decided upon, and I did not wish to take Jack up on his generous proposition until it was. As soon as I had a viable business prospect, this was subject to change.

Ironically, that viable business opportunity would come courtesy of the Jackrabbit himself. It happened on a hunting expedition for some duck decoys Jack had heard about in my hometown of El Sobrante, in San Francisco's East Bay. Jack was already seventy-three years old, but he was able to give me a run for my money, getting up at dawn every morning ready for another day of searching, bargaining, buying, and selling.

On that morning in 1991, Jack and I made for the home of a local decoy collector named Bert Williams. We had about $5,000 in cash, just in case Bert was in the selling mood. Ringing the doorbell in a modest suburban neighborhood, we were greeted by Bert's daughter Kerry and invited in. While Jack and Bert partook of the preliminary pleasantries, I chatted with Kerry, a charming young lady who was excited about the new pickup truck she had just bought and asked if I would like to see it. I was impressed by the shiny new vehicle in the garage, which seemed to have all the bells and whistles. When I asked how she could afford such luxury, she laughed, "I certainly couldn't do it on my teacher's salary. Actually, I have to sell an old guitar to help with the down payment."

My ears perked up. "I, um, know a little about old guitars," I said, trying to keep the excitement out of my voice. "What kinda guitar is it?"

"It's an old 1957 Fender Stratocaster," she replied. "I've been offered five grand for it."

That was pretty much market value for a Stratocaster of that year at that time, so I thought Kerry was getting a fair price. Still, the Strat was my favorite guitar. I wanted to at least get a look at it, so I told Kerry I might be interested in buying it myself.

"It's not here," she said. "It's over at a friend's house; he's helping me sell it." Not to be deterred, I inquired whether it was possible to drop in on her friend. "Well, it's all the way out in Benicia," she said, referring to a town about twenty miles distant. "We could call, but I don't think it's worth the trouble. It's probably been sold by now, anyway. We have a buyer lined up in Florida. But thanks for your interest."

There was something about this story that did not sound right. Why did she have someone else selling the guitar? And why was it not being sold locally? After all, there were plenty of guitar collectors here in California. But what Kerry told me next made it seem certain that this old Strat not only existed but was a special rarity in the world of guitars.

"Florida, eh?" I mused, trying to sound disinterested.

"Yeah," she nodded. "The guy wants it for his collection because it's a white one."

"White?" I asked. "The body of the guitar is white?"

"Yeah," she answered with a shrug. "Is that important?"

Indeed it was. The color of these vintage guitars can be a key component of their value. Even more important is the originality of the finish. The rarer the color (assuming the finish is original), the more valuable the guitar. A white or "blonde" original 1957 Fender Stratocaster is an exceedingly rare instrument, extremely desirable, and certainly more valuable than the $5,000 that Kerry had been offered. In fact, in all my years of collecting and trading guitars to that point, I had never actually laid eyes on an original blonde 1957 Strat. I knew they existed, and now I was on the trail of one . . . or at least I thought I was.

Right then, we were interrupted by Jack and Bert, who wanted me to come in and check out the decoys they were already haggling over. I hemmed and hawed, unwilling to let Kerry out of my sight. She was my link to the white Strat, and, like Captain Ahab and that white whale, I was going to land this mythical creature, come hell or high water.

I mentioned the guitar in passing to Bert to see if he could confirm its existence. "Oh, yass," he immediately replied. "I bought it for Kerry from a neighbor way back in 1968. Yass, I think the original owner had got it brand spankin' new at the Scalise Music Center out there in Richmond." Another piece of the puzzle had fallen into place; it was all starting to add up.

I asked Kerry if there was any possibility I could see the guitar right away. "Call the guy up and let Mike talk to him," the Jackrabbit suggested, instinctively sensing that I was onto a golden—or rather, white—opportunity. Kerry obliged, picking up a phone and calling her friend. "Hi, it's Kerry," she said. "I have a guy here who's interested in the guitar." She passed me the old lime-green telephone from the other room that was connected via a twenty-foot cord. "His name is Ron."

As it turned out, Ron, a friendly chap who did not seem to have a hidden agenda, confirmed everything. He had a buyer in Florida lined up, a fellow named Craig Brodie, whom I knew as a dealer and a collector of Fender guitars. This was a potential roadblock, but I was not about to let it slow me down. Vintage guitar collecting can be a cutthroat business, especially between dealers. Just being the first one to uncover a rare instrument does not mean you have any prior claim. The deal is in play until money changes hands or a contract is agreed upon orally or in writing. So I suggested to Ron that he let me come over and look at the Strat, hinting that, if I liked it, I could pay him in cash and save the hassle, risk, and expense of shipping it across the country.

But Ron was not biting. "I told Mr. Brodie that he could have first crack at the guitar for $5,000," he told me. "He's sending me a contract and a check." He paused for a moment before adding, "Shoot, if it falls through, I'll let you know, but I've already made arrangements with him." Fire and brimstones! That was not good news. I wanted that guitar. After parting with more than a few of my most treasured instruments to pay for room, board, books, and tuition over the course of eight years in the academic wilderness, it was time to start getting those guitars back. And this white Strat could be the beginning—a lucky talisman to revitalize my collector's mojo.

I was ready to vent my frustration into the phone when, just in time, the mantra of my other mentor, Bill Mori, came to mind: "Establish a rapport, number one!" Taking a deep breath, I ventured a few casual questions about Ron's interest in guitars. "Are you a guitar player, Ron?" I finally asked, coming up with what should have been the obvious opener. "Well, yes," he replied. "It's my favorite hobby." As our conversation continued, the voice on the other end of the line began to warm up. The defensive nature subsided.

Quizzed about his musical tastes, Ron offhandedly informed me that he had been in a high school band with a guy who had collected vintage guitars. "Who's that?" I asked. When he said my name I exclaimed, "Wait a minute—that's me!" Unbelievably, I was talking with one of my best friends from high school. I'd failed to recognize that the voice on the other end of the phone belonged to the same fellow I had briefly played with in a group during my salad days of high school music. I had not seen my old friend Ron Garcia in years. We quickly reminisced about how at seventeen we had just been getting our musical bearings, having more fun making noise than actually making music. It had been fourteen years since I had seen this erstwhile musical friend.

"Mike," Ron urged me, "get over here and check out this guitar. This guy in Florida wants it badly, but as long as the check is 'in the mail,' I guess I can still sell it to you." I didn't need an engraved invitation. The Jackrabbit and I sped to Benicia, where Ron was waiting with the guitar. It was even better than he had promised. It was indeed a 1957 Fender Stratocaster, with a serial number of 22227. It had a blonde see-through finish that highlighted the gorgeous grain of its ash body. All in all, it was a magnificent instrument, one of the finest Stratocasters I had ever laid eyes on. I bought the guitar on the spot, paying what we agreed was a fair price. It was not just a very special guitar that we stumbled onto that morning. I reconnected with my old pal, Ron Garcia, who remains a dear friend to this day.

The guitar had the added bonus, in a personal sense, of having been purchased brand new at the Scalise Music Center in nearby Richmond in 1957. This was the same music store where, back in the seventies, I had taken my first guitar lesson. And it was only a few blocks from where my father's used car lot was in the fifties. I subsequently took the guitar to Tony Scalise, the store's retired owner, to help establish its provenance. He remembered special-ordering the instrument for a customer in 1957. Inside the case were some old postcards picturing the Scalise Music store in its prime. "They sure don't make them like this anymore," Tony said, carefully inspecting the vintage Strat. No truer words were ever spoken.

Something else significant had occurred at the Williams house that day. In a flash, it was confirmed that there were still old guitars out there, stashed under beds, in closets, attics, and dusty garages. Contrary to what most guitar collectors thought—that all the best instruments had already been snapped up and that from now on it was a game between dealers—it became clear to me in the most direct way that there were still treasures left to unearth. On that day the die was cast, once and for all, for me to devote myself to hunting down vintage guitars. It was a clarion call, loud and clear. And my answer was to be unmistakable. As we drove home with that prized guitar and a satisfied sense of a job well done, the Jackrabbit turned to me and said with a smile, "I guess you have a good reason to borrow that fifty grand now."

3

VAN HORN, TEXAS

That summer of '91 was my crossroads. I had finally completed my postgraduate and law degrees and could make a "sensible" career move or take a shot on the, shall we say, less predictable world of vintage guitar dealing. "I'll just do this for a few more months," I kept mumbling to myself as the weather warmed and I felt the urge to hit the road, "and then I'll start sending out my resume." But finding that blonde 1957 Fender Stratocaster that had been sitting under a bed for twenty-five years in my own hometown persuaded me to give the guitar business a try.

Before I knew it, my "guitar summer" had lasted over a year. Every week I would exclaim, "Soon, very soon I shall buckle down and find serious work. Soon!" Making a living buying and selling vintage guitars—it seemed about as incongruous as it would be for a high school dropout to get hired as a brain surgeon. Still, somehow, I could just never get to the point of folding up my tent and calling it quits. I had borrowed that $50,000 from my friend Jack Ruggles and had paid it back, with interest, within ninety days. Now I had my own working capital.

Yet I was certainly not getting any closer to a traditional career by scouring the large and small towns of America on an obsessive guitar safari, searching for those collectible guitars. That's why I swore, in the waning months of 1992, that I would definitely get back on a career track—right after the big ol' guitar show in Dallas, Texas.

The annual Texas Guitar Show was the largest anywhere. More than 10,000 people crowded in from across the globe to buy and sell some of the world's most coveted vintage guitars. For the occasion, I decided on one last road trip, loading my trusty van with prime examples from my burgeoning collection. I planned to turn a profit and perhaps, even more tantalizing, make some advantageous trades. This was to be my last road trip, the final guitar hurrah.

When friend and fellow musician and guitar collector Mike Parker asked if he could tag along on the ride from California, I immediately agreed. I thought it would be nice to have some company on the three-day tour. (And yes, somehow the lyrics *"Just sit right back and you'll hear a tale, a tale of a fateful trip . . ."* came to my mind.)

In a way, traveling with Mike Parker was rather like being stranded with Gilligan on the desert isle. As you can imagine, we had a lot to talk about on our long road trip through the empty desert landscape of the arid Southwest. Our conversation, or should I say Mike's nonstop questions, inevitably turned to the means and methods I used to get my hands on the great vintage guitars I had been finding. Even back then, I had a reputation among my peers for miraculously uncovering rare and well-preserved guitars, often at most reasonable prices.

My technique could not have been simpler. All it required was a lot of hard work and the willingness to travel to some very out-of-the-way locations. My first step was to run radio and print advertisements seeking guitars for sale throughout the country. As responses to the ads came in, I methodically followed through, no matter how far I might have to journey. Eventually, as my business grew, I compiled a database of possible purchases based on those ads, word of mouth, and rumors on the guitar-collecting grapevine. That database today holds over ten thousand leads.

Any guitar dealer could figure this out, providing he had the time, determination, and taste for travel required to follow up the leads, but I was not about to give away my trade secrets, as straightforward as they might have been. Monsieur Parker had tried his best to crack my resolute silence. During the seemingly endless miles from the Bay Area to Dallas, he would ask at regular intervals, "So where are you getting all these guitars, man?" I would nod and smile and babble something vague, but when we crossed the New Mexico border into the Lone Star State, he abruptly ran out of patience.

"I want to know, chief!" he insisted, and I immediately sensed the opportunity to have a little fun with my friend.

"Mike," I told him in my best conspiratorial whisper, "I'm going to show you how it's done. But you can't tell anybody how I do this—ever. You understand?"

He readily agreed (perhaps a bit too readily). "I won't tell nobody."

My plan was simple and, if I say so myself, delightfully insincere. As we passed the outskirts of El Paso on the I-10, I pulled off at the next exit in that vast heartland. I was determined to take Mike on a wild goose chase he would never forget, to discourage him once and for all from ever pursuing vintage guitar collecting using the "Guitar Man" method.

"What the hell are we doing here?" Mike asked as we turned off the freeway and cruised down the main street of that skinny strip of dusty Texas. The windblown hamlet of Van Horn looked like a mid-twentieth-century ghost town, a vista from a past era, or a stage set left over from *The Last Picture Show*.

The forlorn town traced its roots to two men named Van Horn. In 1849, U.S. Army Major Jefferson Van Horn was en route to a command at Fort Bliss in El Paso, a U.S. stronghold against the Native Americans in the region. He stumbled across drinking water twelve miles south of the main drag we were now driving, and the Van Horn Wells became an important stop on the Old Spanish Trail.

The second Van Horn was the affable, beloved Lt. James Judson Van Horn, no relation to the first. The town was named after him in 1881, the year the last link in the Texas & Pacific Railroad was complete. Its proximity to the tracks made Van Horn a watering hole for steam engines carrying freight and passengers to and from the new frontier.

When Interstate 10 was built, the town was more or less by-passed and, contrary to the glowing description in the Chamber of Commerce brochure we picked up, became maybe the most desolate habitation in the whole of that empty quarter of Texas. All of which was going to work to my distinct advantage that day . . . or so I thought. I relished the mystified look Mike gave me as I parked in front of a ramshackle old mom-and-pop hardware store.

"You want guitars?" I asked, clicking off the ignition. "Watch and learn, padre."

Opening the flyspecked screen door, we were greeted by an elderly gentleman straight out of a casting call for *Mayberry R.F.D.* This clerk was a wiry, insect-like man dressed in what appeared to be an old gas attendant uniform, complete with a bow tie and the most dilapidated yellow leather boots I had ever seen. An old white plastic name badge gloriously revealed his name, which was embossed on an even older-looking "Dymo" label tag.

"Excuse me . . . I'm wondering if you might know of any guitar players in these parts, Snark," I asked casually, as Mike watched intently over my shoulder.

The old codger squinted at us over his wire-rimmed glasses. "*Mister* Snark," he corrected. "Where'd you fellers say you were from?" he asked with more than a hint of small-town suspicion.

We had not said, but I knew better than to mention the city of San Francisco out here in the heart of redneck America. "We're from Gold Country out in California, Mister Snark," I said deferentially, hoping it would conjure a familiar image of grubby miners from the Old West.

It seemed to work. "And what brings you out our way?" the clerk asked, in a decidedly friendlier tone.

"Well," I replied, "I'm a big fan of your old-time guitar music. You know, the cowpoke stuff from the fifties and even back before then. The days when music was music. I know that some of the best of it came out of Texas and I was just wondering if there might be some of those old guitar pickers still around these parts."

There was a long pause as the good old boy cast his mind back to those long-forgotten days. "Ummm, guitars," he said at last. "Well there is one old fella named Frank. He used to run the only music outfit we ever had here in Van Horn. Don't know if he's doin' any pickin' these days, but he still lives in a little place above the old store. He used to sell all sorts of stuff in there: harmonicas, accordions, guitars, and guns, too, if I recall correctly." He pointed with his thumb over his shoulder. "Last two-story building we got here in town on Main—that's the north side as you're leavin'. Can't miss it."

This wasn't working out exactly as I had planned. Intending to show Mike just how desperately hard and seemingly hopeless finding vintage guitars could be, I instead might have stumbled onto a hidden cache of the real thing. I tried to contain my excitement as I thanked the clerk. Just as we were walking out the door he cautioned:

"Oh, one last thing, partner: Frank's got a pretty grand-daughter, just 'bout yer age. But boy, ya' gotta steer clear. I hear she's nuttier than a squirrel turd."

"Ummm . . . okay, Mister Snark . . . no problemo!" I shouted as we climbed back into the van, heading for the edge of town.

I took a deep breath. Chances were this was nothing more than a dead end. I had encountered more than a few of them in my travels. I was ready for anything. But Mike Parker was counting the chickens before they had hatched—or even had been laid, for that matter. "Damn, an old guitar store!" said Mike, astounded, shaking his head. His admiration for me doubled. If this was all it took, no wonder I was making such a killing find-ing old guitars, and he wasn't.

"Just another day at the office," I intoned, not sure whether I had outsmarted him or myself. "But the granddaughter sure sounds intriguing."

Just as the old Snark had said, we found the two-story build-ing at the edge of town: a shabby brick storefront with a tiny apartment behind it up a flight of stairs. With the store win-dows blacked out by newspaper, it was clear no business had been conducted there for years. While Mike waited in the van, I trudged up the rickety stairs and knocked on the apartment door. There was no answer, so I knocked again. I was about to give up when the door creaked open and a small, weathered old man greeted me in the thickest Texas drawl I had ever heard.

"Wh'sha wunt?" I think he said. As I stated my business, he fixed me with an appraising squint. Then, to my utter amaze-ment, he pointed downstairs to the back entrance of the store, beckoning me to proceed. Could this be happening? Who knew what vintage treasures lurked behind that dilapidated doorway?

Mike, meanwhile, had caught sight of us and hurried to join the festivities. Now, my friend Mike, a.k.a. "the Bug," was a twitchy, heavyset gentleman of Native American ancestry with an insatiable thirst for Dr. Pepper. With his ponytail and camouflage military fatigues he looked a little like an outlaw biker, or maybe a little like a paramilitary nut job. All right, he looked like your average psycho killer, but he was harmless enough. I do believe that he gave old Frank the heebie-jeebies. Perhaps it was just the machete-sized knife that Mike always had strapped to his belt.

I explained that Mike was one of those rock 'n' roll guitar players, well intentioned and well known back on the coast. This didn't seem to calm Frank much, but nevertheless, with that he opened the creaky door to the old store and we anxiously crowded in. It looked like a Texas twister had blown through the cramped space. Debris was piled to the ceiling. The only breeze stirring the heavy pall of dust carried an aroma of rat excrement and old cardboard. As we pulled newspapers off windows to get a better look, there was not a guitar in sight.

"See," I almost said to Mike, "it's not as easy as it looks." This was turning out to be just another false lead. Or was it? The two of us started poking around as old Frank made a path through the trash toward the back of the store. There, a shapeless pile covered with blue plastic tarps loomed large in a far corner.

Mike and I simultaneously saw that something was stashed beneath the corners of those stained and grungy tarps. Before I could take a step, Mike headed to that pile in a beeline. For a big, slow-moving guy he apparently had a lot of speed when he needed it. High-stepping it like former Dallas Cowboys running back Emmitt Smith on the five-yard line, he ducked and weaved through a defensive line of old boxes and random rubbish. He arrived at the pile just as Frank, with a feeble flourish, pulled back the first tarp.

We could not believe our eyes. There, under a thick layer of grime, was a stack of classic Fender "tweed" guitar amplifiers, every one collectible and quite valuable. That was only the beginning. As our host pulled back a second and then a third tarp, a stack of guitar cases—perhaps twenty in all—was revealed, radiating a halo of vintage splendor. I knew immediately what was in those cases. Unfortunately, so did Mike. Old Frank stood there surveying the scene. A bright ray of blue light pierced the dust-laden room and made the old fellow's milky-brown eyes blink as the dank particles hung in the air. This was the moment of truth.

Before Frank could even open the latches on the first case, Mike grabbed it and barked, "How much you want for this?" At this moment your humble narrator wanted to swat the Bug. The first rule of guitar negotiation—or *any* negotiation—is not to show your hand too early. If the old Texan got wind we were as excited as Mike foolishly let on, he was sure to drive a harder bargain. "I got plenty of cash," Mike foolishly blurted out. "Plenty of cash." And if I said one word of caution to Mike about this ill-timed outburst . . . well, the ball game would be over before it started. Under those circumstances, any old trader worth his salt would hold out for more money—or, worse, not sell at all. My only option was to defuse the sticky situation by walking to the other side of the store to casually inspect some old crates.

From there I watched with increasing dismay as Mr. Cool Breeze in camo opened one case after another, proclaiming, "Wow, I'll take it!" or "Whoo, that's nice!" or "Yuup! Sold!" Sold? He hadn't even negotiated the asking price yet.

Mike was clearly mucking up the potential for a great deal on some choice guitars. And, to be quite candid, it didn't feel so good to get cut out of my own find. But I had one ace in the hole, one little advantage the Bug lacked: money—good old U.S. currency. I knew my friend was short on bread, since he'd asked me at the beginning of our trip to lend him some if he found something he liked at the guitar show. So I had a strong hunch he would be putting the bite on me for money right about this time. Sure enough, a few minutes later he turned to me, wide-eyed with enthusiasm.

"Hey man, I'm buying these guitars," he said. "I need to borrow some money."

I nodded toward the front door. "It's out in the car . . ." and then hinted broadly, "Why don't you come out with me to get it?"

"No," he demurred, eyes still on the trove of guitars. "I'll wait here."

"Mike," I said forcefully, "Come with me."

As irritated as I was, it was hard to stay mad at Mike. Never having been in such a potentially lucrative situation, he'd showed his hand way too early in this game. As a guitar "picker" it is axiomatic that you never lose your cool, and never let them see you sweat. Never. But right then, Mike was not interested in learning anything, except how much money I would front him.

"Hey, Mike," I calmly admonished him back at the van. "This is my lead. I told you that I would show you how it's done. I didn't say I would give you the lead or let you buy the guitars with my money. I've got first crack at these guitars, and unless you back off, ain't squat happenin' here, brother. You've already tipped this guy off that he's sitting on a freakin' gold mine."

"Aww, hell, no" was his predictable yet adamant reply. "There are at least ten of those that are already mine. You can buy them from me afterwards if you want. But you know . . . first come, first served, Holmes."

At that moment, the adage of the great German philosopher Friedrich Nietzsche came to mind: "Battle not with monsters lest ye become one." Yet that calming precept was soon overcome by one propounded by a great Italian thinker, Don Vito Corleone. I decided therefore to make Mike "an offer he could not refuse." I stepped forward and said, "Do you know what Lightnin' Hopkins meant when he said 'the rubber on a wheel is faster than the rubber on the heel'?" At that moment, Mike looked at me like a boxer sitting in his corner, being lectured to after a bad round. "It's still about five hundred miles from here to Dallas," I said, "so you choose: it's my way or the highway."

Mike became as jittery as a mad rattlesnake. There was a brief staredown.

He hissed, spat, kicked the dirt, wiped his face, and thought about it for a long minute. He finally said, "Ahhh, shit! You win." The message had gotten through. To soothe his feelings, I assured him that I would give him second pick of the litter and would even loan him the money to buy a guitar or two. Mike did not like it, but what choice did he have? We quickly returned as a united front to conclude our business with old Frank.

The twenty-plus guitars and amplifiers we purchased were in superb condition. Mostly part of Frank's old inventory, they had never been sold. In guitar parlance, such items are known as "new old stock," the most desirable objects of vintage guitar collectors. Among the selections we made, most had been manufactured in the seventies. That's not the most highly coveted collectible guitar era, but as they were top name brands—Fender, Gibson, and Rickenbacker—we walked away very pleased with our acquisitions. I like to think Frank had a good day, too, converting old, languishing stock into several fat stacks of hundred-dollar bills. As we shut the door on the now stuffed van, I turned to Frank, shook his hand, and said ominously, "I'll be back."

Before we left Van Horn, we also returned to the hardware store and thanked Mister Snark, in the form of a crisp C-note. As we drove away, Mike said, "And we never got to meet the wacko-bird granddaughter." I started to say, "Maybe next trip," but I stopped. "Damn shame," I said instead. "Damn shame."

We ended up selling almost everything we'd bought in Van Horn at the guitar show, making a tidy profit. And, while Mike now knew all about my "secret" method of finding vintage guitars in the field, he was never able to follow up. It was just too much hard work and travel for a tightly wound guy like Mike. More important, that trip proved to be the coup de grace for my corporate career. The summer hiatus of 1991 had turned into a permanent reprieve from the ranks of button-down America. This "guitar summer" turned out to be an endless one.

4

SWEET HOME OKLAHOMA

Bill Mori, my duck decoy–collecting mentor, taught me the tricks of the trade: how to advertise in newspapers, work a room for maximum effect, and always ask one critical question before saying goodbye: "Do you know anybody else who has any decoys?" If the reply was "Yes," as it often was, I had a new lead. Just as Bill had done, I would pursue these tips to the ends of the earth—or at least as long as my gasoline held out.

One day in 1993, Jack "the Jackrabbit" Ruggles was employing this technique. "There's an old guy down here in a bar in San Pablo," he informed me, "who's got some decoys that I went to take a gander at. When I was down there, I asked 'im if he had any old geetars, because I saw that he had one hung up on the wall. He told me he had an ol' Fender and 'n ol' Martin. Ya' better get yer ass down here."

San Pablo was not far. I jumped in my car and was there within the hour. Searching for the address, I approached what appeared to be a saloon in an old part of the venerable working-class town. It was a magnificent establishment. Once inside, I walked up to Jack and he immediately introduced me to an old-timer—polishing shot glasses behind the bar—by the name of Joseph "Jody" Dellacourt.

"Hi, Jody, I hear you've got some guitars," I said, as casually as possible.

"Yup," was his laconic reply. "I got a couple, but I'm too busy 'round here to show them to ya' now. If ya' can hang around for half 'n hour or so, we can talk."

"Fine," I said, settling on a barstool and sipping a Coke while surveying the joint. Jack finished his soda water and departed. There were a handful of wet regulars who might as well have been boozing it up in that old public house since the Great Depression. They were nursing drinks and staring at soap operas on a flickering TV bolted to a high corner of the dark room. Next to the TV was a row of stuffed birds—mostly pheasants and ducks that looked like they had been there for fifty years. They had all turned a dark, syrupy brown color, having been ensconced in that nicotine-filled atmosphere for decades.

It was a dive bar, no doubt, but Jody seemed to take a lot of pride in his seedy establishment. The place might not have changed a lick since the 1950s, but it was a neat, tidy reflection of the proprietor himself. A thin man with tortoiseshell glasses, Jody wore his gray hair slicked back with Dapper Dan pomade. He wore a clean white apron on top of an immaculately maintained suit with a vintage forties cut. But as time passed, Jody threw me perturbed looks. I chalked that up to the fact that I was sticking with my single glass of soda pop. A half-hour passed, and then an hour, and he seemed no more inclined to move out from behind his bar than when I first arrived.

"Can you give me some idea of what you've got?" I asked politely, trying to get the ball rolling. He hung up his hand towel, took a deep breath, and gave me a wry grin. There must have been something in my expression that suggested that my own

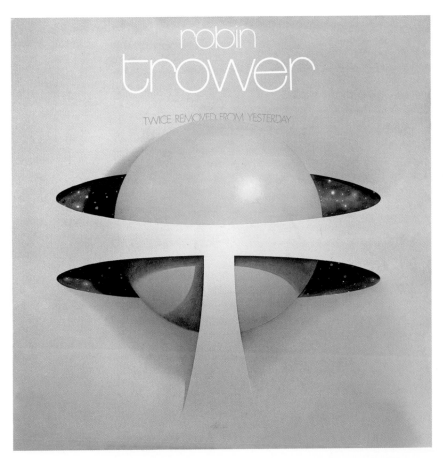

The first album I ever purchased was Robin Trower's first, *Twice Removed from Yesterday* (1973). Well worth the long bicycle ride to buy it! It led to my first rock concert, seeing Trower perform on March 14, 1975. (Author's collection)

LEFT: The Winterland Arena, an iconic San Francisco music hall, was the site of the Trower concert and the birthplace of my desire to play guitar. (Photo by Chris Horn)

BOTTOM: Robin Trower sporting his trusty 1956 Stratocaster at the Winterland concert that changed the course of my life. (Photo copyright Jim Marshall Photography, LLC)

Me with my first vintage guitar, a 1955 Fender Stratocaster, circa 1976. It looked and sounded just like Trower's Strat. Note my Trower T-shirt showing Robin playing his 1956 Strat. (Author's collection)

I bought this rare
blonde 1957 Fender
Stratocaster, serial
number 22227,
in 1991 with help
from my friend
Ron Garcia. Notice
the grainy ash
wood body detail.
(Author's collection)

Scalise Music, in Richmond, California, circa 1960s—where the blonde Stratocaster was sold new in 1957, and where I took my first music lesson in 1976. (Author's collection)

Mike Parker, a.k.a. "the Bug," travel companion and fellow guitar collector. Mike is holding a 1958 Explorer that I sold him. This guitar was once owned by Don Preston, a guitarist that played with Leon Russell. (Photo by Michael J. Parker)

My grandfather Bill Scoggins (top right) and his close friend Jody Dellacourt (bottom center), in Point Richmond, California, circa 1943. A lead on vintage guitars resulted, incredibly, in my chance meeting with Jody—fifty years later. (Author's collection)

A publicity photo of Bob Wills and his Texas Playboys, circa 1960s. Grandpa Bill once toured with Wills but got the boot after losing a showdown with another fiddle player who wanted his job. (Courtesy of the Bob Wills Museum)

Bill Scoggins (center) and me (far right), in 1973. (Author's collection)

A 1950 "Nocaster," one of the rarest and most collectible Fenders. "Nocasters" were actually Broadcasters (Fender's first electric Spanish-style guitars), but when a lawsuit forced the company to drop the name, the decals were trimmed back to read simply "Fender." (Author's collection)

patience was waning, because he finally got down to business. He had an old Telecaster, he told me, which, to the best of his knowledge, had been made back in the 1950s.

"You don't say," I mused, underplaying my interest. "Well, I might be interested in that. Can I take a look at it?"

Now it was Jody's turn to feign disinterest. "Could be," he replied. "Course, it ain't here. Keep it back home. Maybe I'll bring her in one day."

You had to admire the old guy; he was certainly playing it close to the pinstriped vest.

"I'm in no hurry whatsoever," I said, "as long as it's no later than tomorrow morning at eight o'clock," deciding it was worth risking my negotiating position a little in order to kick the can down the road and rattle the old-timer a bit.

Jody chortled and allowed that he might think about that, but in the meantime, I had noticed something special about this old character. Perhaps, I calculated, there was more than one way to get him to open up.

"That's an interesting accent you've got there, Jody." It was indeed, somewhere between a Texas drawl and an Arkansas twang. "If I had to guess, I'd say you were from Oklahoma or thereabouts."

Jody's eyebrows arched and it was clear that I had guessed right. He was doing his best to hide his surprise, but I had finally gotten around his standoffish defense.

But just then, one of the older patrons who had been eavesdropping from far down the bar interjected himself into the situation.

"Jody, you ain't gonna sell your get-tar, are ya'? 'Cause I got a friend who buys 'em. I'll bet he'll snap her right up. I'll call 'im up right now if ya' want."

Great! Now some drunk was attempting to scotch my deal

[pun intended] while trying to make points with the bartender in one inebriated fell swoop.

"Hey, mister," I said, "are you trying to help me out? 'Cause if you are, next time I need your help, I'll ask for it."

The man got up and, without even looking my way, wobbled over to the jukebox, where I could hear him dropping in quarters . . . a whole lot of quarters. Based on his attire, I inferred he was going to play some fine western music. And he exceeded all expectations. The first song was Dolly Parton's magnum opus, "Nine to Five." Jody had pretended not to hear the old drunk's comments, as bartenders are formally trained to do. Eventually Jody turned back to me, and just as he did, "Okie from Muskogee" dropped on the jukebox turntable with a loud thump and began to play. The old drunk who'd played it looked right at me as he sang sloppily along to the verse, *"White lightnin's still the biggest thrill of all . . ."*

"That's right, son," Jody said.

"What's right?" I asked, not sure if Jody was agreeing with me or with Merle Haggard's lyrics.

"I've got relatives from Oklahoma."

Now the drunk was singing louder: *"I'm proud to be an Okie from Muskogee . . ."*

Over the din of the crooner, I loudly let Jody know that we had something in common. "My grandfather was from a little town called Stigler, in Oklahoma."

Jody's rheumy old eyes lit up. He reached down and apparently hit some magic button to turn the music down, because the jukebox went cold, and so did our barroom troubadour.

"Stigler? Jesus H. Christ," he replied.

At last I had Jody's full attention.

"Yeah," I said, "Stigler's just about an hour from Okemah, Oklahoma, the place Woody Guthrie was from. I reckon that my grandpa was cut from the same cloth as guys like Woody Guthrie and Will Rogers. He sure loved music."

"I'm from Stigler myself!" Jody shot back. "Came out here back in nineteen and forty-one to work in the shipyards during the war."

Now it was my turn to be surprised.

"My granddad came out in '41, too," I exclaimed. "He worked at the shipyards as well. Maybe you knew him; his name was Bill Scoggins."

Jody's grizzled jaw dropped. "Bill Scoggins," he whispered with the chill of old memories in his voice. He looked like he'd seen a ghost. "D'you say Scoggins or Scroggins?"

"Scoggins—no R," I replied.

"Bill Scoggins was my best friend!"

We stared at each other for a long moment, both of us stunned at this remarkable possible coincidence. Then Jody, still in disbelief, inundated me with a flood of questions: Where had Scoggins lived? What had he done with himself since the shipyard days? What was my grandmother's name? Just as we seemed to resolve the matter the old drunk rejoined the discourse.

"Jody, can you put my damn music back on?" he implored.

"Damn it, Lester," Jody said, "will ya' just give me a minute here? It's important, okay?"

Whatever doubts I had that we were talking about the same Bill Scoggins disappeared within minutes when Jody reached into a drawer and pulled out a pile of faded old photographs. Shuffling through them as fast as a Vegas card dealer, he stopped when he found one picture in particular and looked hard at it. When he handed it to me I saw the unmistakable image of my grandfather and Jody in the 1940s standing together with several other men in front of a bar. There was no doubt:

Jody was my grandfather's close friend from way back in Stigler, Oklahoma.

As it turned out, they had grown up together in the ecological and human disaster of the Oklahoma Dust Bowl of the 1930s. I was quickly filled in on their history. They had come west together to work in the shipyards and then gone into business during the war, setting up a saloon they dubbed the Roma Bar in Point Richmond, California. It was a familiar name. My mother used to tell me tales of that same rough juke joint when I was a kid. After recounting this story, Jody finally turned the music back up. But I wasn't about to leave, not now. I ordered a Budweiser and must have warmed that old red barstool for another two hours.

As memories poured forth in the lengthening afternoon shadows Jody kept saying "Son of a bitch," shaking his head in disbelief. "I can't believe I'm sittin' here with Bill Scoggins' grandson."

The next time we met, a few weeks later, Jody pulled out more photographs from the era, many depicting my grandfather. None of those snapshots had ever been seen by my family. The fact was, any memento of my grandfather was precious to us. Besides his family, which included six children, he never really had many close friends in California—except, as it turned out, for Jody. Eventually, I brought my mother down to meet her father's best buddy. When Jody saw her for the first time in fifty-five years, he recognized my mother without hesitation. "You don't change!" he exclaimed.

Despite the excitement, I didn't forget what I had come to see. "I still want a look at that guitar," I reminded him. Jody grinned, "You're just like your grandfather. Single-minded son of a bitch." The next day he brought the guitar from his home.

It was worth the wait: a 1959 Telecaster in virtually mint

condition, with the original rich and patina yellowed blonde finish.

"I want to buy it, Jody," I told him after I had given it a careful once-over. "Why don't you shoot me a price?"

He hesitated. Jody was sentimental—but no sentimental fool. Our common bond notwithstanding, he was not about to hand over the beautiful 1959 Telecaster for old times' sake. "I'll have to ask my wife," he told me. "It kind-lee belongs to the two of us."

A few days later he got back to me with the news that his wife wouldn't part with it. Too many memories were attached. "But Jody," I pleaded, giving him my hardest sell, "that's just the point. It's got sentimental value for me, too. The way we met—your friendship with my grandfather . . . The guitar is a link between you and me, and between us and my grandpappy. Besides, you can't even play the damn thing!"

Jody ruefully shook his head. "Can't do it," he said. "I hear what you're sayin' . . . I wish I could, but the ol' lady would kill me if I let it go. You can come visit it anytime you want, though."

I sighed, eliciting a promise that, if he ever decided to part with the Telecaster, I'd get the first chance to buy it. He agreed, and I had to be satisfied that, even if I had not scored that pristine and valuable instrument for my collection, I had unearthed an amazing piece of family history. Naturally, I kept in touch with Jody, dropping in to see him regularly and just as regularly reminding him of his promise to give me first crack at the guitar if he and his wife should ever decide to sell.

Then, just a year after we had met, I got a call from Jody's daughter with the sad news that Jody had died of a sudden heart attack. Even though Jody was up in age, it still came as a shock. I attended the funeral services and, amidst the prayers and eulogies, considered myself lucky to have met that old character and to have heard firsthand all the stories about him, my grandfather, and their rough times together. It had been a relationship that began with an amazing happenstance.

A few weeks after the services, Jody's wife called, hinting heavily that she wanted to talk about the guitar. "I know he wanted you to have it," she informed me, and said it could at last be mine for $7,000. My initial offer to Jody had been $4,000. The fact was, at $4,000, I was offering to pay market value at the time; $7,000 was steep. I was more than a little taken aback that she was asking such a high price. What I had told Jody was the truth; more than anything I just wanted the Telecaster for its sentimental value. "Let me think about it," I said, but that turned out to be the last time I ever talked to her.

To this day, I consider that Fender one of the ones that got away: a great guitar with a personal story that came to light completely by accident. I went looking for a guitar and met my grandfather's best friend. Had Jody's Telecaster actually become mine, would I have hung onto it just for the pleasure of taking it out and telling the tale of that San Pablo bar and its anachronistic owner? Yes, I think so.

But the musical connection between my grandfather and me did not stop with Jody. In a truly remarkable manner, his life and legacy kept appearing in the most unexpected places among the most unlikely people.

5

TEXAS PLAYBOY

For the first year, my collecting excursions were pretty much confined to the San Francisco Bay Area. My mother's fiancé had given me his brown 1980 Pontiac Phoenix to use in my guitar pursuits. Now, this was a fine little vehicle, but it certainly was not designed for the transnational guitar dealer that I aspired to be. I eventually put over 200,000 miles on the small hatchback. I would go on major guitar trips and return with guitars stacked to her roof.

One time I recall heading north on Interstate 5, on Southern California's treacherous "Grapevine," while returning to San Francisco from a Los Angeles buying trip. The mighty Phoenix was so loaded down with guitars that cars were passing me like I was standing still. A friendly member of the California Highway Patrol noticed my slow progress and decided to pull me over. He warned me about "impeding traffic." When he saw that I had a full load of vintage guitars, he said, "Try not to go so slow. And, umm, do you have any old Telecasters for sale?"

Yes, I needed a more suitable vehicle that would allow me to expand my guitar travels outside the Bay Area, but my obsession for adding the next guitar to my collection was actually hampering my ability to go nationwide as a guitar hunter. It was just hard for me to let go of the cash to purchase a new van—because I knew that as soon as I did, a great guitar would present itself and then I would not have the resources to buy it!

By the mid-nineties, my advertising network had expanded to all of California and many other states. "There are guitars all over this country," I kept telling myself. With that, I finally threw down for a new van and retired the proud Phoenix. Now, with the resources to open up the search area, I ran ads on everything from TV and radio to the community bulletin boards of mobile home parks. The net was cast across New Mexico, Texas, Colorado, all the way to New Jersey, touching every point in between.

Based on the responses, I would venture out on buying trips that often lasted for weeks. It was not unusual to return from those treasure hunts with fifty or sixty guitars, which would be sold to finance the next road trip, keeping back a few prime instruments for the collection. For six years—from 1992 to 1998—I lived largely on the road and gave up much to get my business started. With no roots, no social life, and no sweetheart, it was just me, a map, and the road as my best friend. My next destinations were marked out based on the leads I was following. That is what you need to do to find the best guitars. It was work that no one else was willing to do, which is why my business really started turning a substantial profit at that time.

Also, my close college friend Serge Wilson helped me create a computer database to track and monitor all of the contacts that I had obtained. It was a decided advantage. Say, for example, that I was heading for Arkansas. Upon arrival in the first town along my route, I would call all the contacts from that area in my database, never forgetting to ask the all-important question— "Do you know anybody else with an old guitar?"—that often generated my next lead. So it was no wonder that, expecting to be gone ten days, I could end up roaming the country for a month. In the same way, plans to come home with twenty guitars could turn into a haul of fifty. In those years it was beautiful to be an obsessive guitar hunter, wandering through states, cities, and towns from coast to coast and border to border. It was exhilarating to be finding and acquiring more vintage instruments than anyone else in the world.

Returning from these expeditions would require the quick turnaround of most of the purchases. I would advertise in guitar magazines to sell the instruments or connect with the network of dealers who would regularly buy them. There were an abundance of outlets through which to sell vintage guitars.

When the Internet came along, it radically changed my business, and did so for many others. Most significantly, the World Wide Web altered the information gap that had worked in my favor. Now, if someone wanted to sell a deceased family member's 1959 Les Paul, she could turn to the Internet and establish the value in minutes. She could find ten different examples of that particular Les Paul for sale, giving a good indication of a guitar's true market value. In the past, her recourse would have been to call a guitar store for an appraisal, a time-consuming process. Even then, often as not, your average guitar store would have no idea what a good instrument was really worth, and that elderly lady would end up with an inaccurate valuation. The Internet changed everything, for better and for worse.

Back in 1995, not that many potential sellers had access to the Web. Take one older gentleman who contacted me from Carlsbad, New Mexico, that year, with information regarding a 1937 D-28 Martin. I duly entered his information into my database and marked Carlsbad as a stop on my next travel itinerary.

When I arrived, I was made welcome by the Martin's owner and his pleasant family. This fellow, who was in his eighties, had a smirk like a Cheshire cat, and a big, loud laugh that you would never forget. As usual, we got to talking and the conversation soon turned to the instrument and the owner's history with it.

"Yeah," he reminisced as he opened the guitar case, "I used to play this D-28 get-tar with Bob Wills and the Texas Playboys."

My twist-of-fate antenna immediately went up. "My grandfather, Bill Scoggins, used to play with Bob Wills, too," I replied as he handed me the guitar. I went on to relate a famous anecdote that was told to me at a young age. "It was back when he was touring with Bob Wills," I began, still holding that prewar Martin. "They showed up for a gig and a fiddle player came up and told Wills, 'I want to join this band.'

"'A lot of people want to join my band,' Wills replied. 'What have you got that they don't?'

"'Well, for one thing,' said the fiddle player, 'I'm better than the fella you got now.'" As I explained to my host, that fella was none other than my grandfather.

Bob Wills supposedly said, "Well, then, let me state it for the record book that if you're better, then why don't ya' get on up there with him on that stage? Whoever gets the most clapping has the job." Never one to back down from a challenge, my grandfather readily agreed to the contest; he had some searing hot fiddle chops himself that he planned to use to dispatch his opponent.

The whole incident was like a precursor to today's smash TV show *American Idol*—winner take all, and sudden death to the loser. In this case, the interloper hit the stage and was true to his word. He raised the roof of that old roadhouse with his fiddle playing. "Sorry, Bill," Bob Wills supposedly lamented, "You're out." My grandfather was shown the door.

As I recounted the story, one of my favorites, my Carlsbad host stared in silence for a few moments, tears welling in his eyes. "I was on tour with Wills that night! Saw it happen. Saw your grandpop lose his job," he said and got to his feet. "Come on, son; make me an offer on that Martin guitar. You were meant to have it sure as I'm standin' here." His smirk and his loud laugh were now gone. It seemed this weird coincidence unfolding in his living room had brought him to realize just how long it had been since he was a young man, playing the western swing circuit.

Aside from that old Martin D-28, he also had a beautiful 1959 Fender Telecaster Custom, a superb-sounding guitar. I bought it on the spot, and it eventually ended up with John Frusciante from the Red Hot Chili Peppers. While the old Martin had some problems, and I perhaps paid too much for it, I felt a real bond with that old Texas Playboy that meant more than just getting my money's worth. Before the day was over I bought a few more instruments from him, along with a hard-to-find 1959 tweed-covered Fender Bassman amp.

One thing I have learned from buying and selling guitars is just how small the world really is. I have also experienced how ironic life can be. While my grandfather's closest friend would not sell me his guitar, a man who'd simply seen a fiddle player lose his gig felt strongly enough to let go of his instruments because of our personal connection and the long-gone memories that were rekindled by our meeting.

6

GIVING THE DOG A BONE

Above and beyond the insane amount of travel required to build and maintain an inventory of vintage guitars, the most difficult part of the process is locating them. Where are they? Who has them?

When I fly across the country, I look down and see the millions of houses dotting the land and I think to myself, "Man, there must be a lot of old guitars in those houses!" As a practical matter, I have to figure out which houses have those guitars. The houses that interest me most were made before the 1970s. Those built in the 1940s and 1950s (or earlier) are most likely to hold stringed treasures because homes and their contents often pass down through one family from generation to generation. And those contents just might include a guitar, perhaps two—or perhaps five! Old vintage guitars, ripe for the picking, sweet old guitars, are sitting in those old houses collecting dust—in attics, in broom closets, under beds, in garages, in basements; they can be just about anywhere. There are hundreds of thousands of these guitars still out there, just waiting to be picked.

But getting in contact with the women and men who have these guitars is truly difficult. I have run thousands of radio and newspaper ads looking for them. I have run ads on cable television and on the Internet. But beyond all of that, my very good friend Serge Wilson helped me brainstorm ways to ferret out these valuable guitars. Serge was my professor's aide while I was an undergraduate at the University of California at Berkeley. After graduating himself from Berkeley with a bachelor's degree in literature, Serge did what anyone who specialized in the rhetoric of Marcus Tullius Cicero would do: he started programming computers.

Mind you, this was back in the days before there was great financial promise in that avocation, but with a brilliant eye toward the future, Mr. Wilson continued to write computer programs—with no formal training and no background in the subject. When finally this idea known as the Internet began to gain currency, Serge was one of the first to comprehend just how much currency was at stake . . . billions. By 1999, Serge D. Wilson was being hailed as an Internet visionary by the *Wall Street Journal* and the *New York Times*. He was even called upon to debate the end of the Internet bubble, where he very correctly predicted the stock market downfall of the sector he had helped to create.

So one fine evening I was having dinner with Serge at a Korean barbeque restaurant in Oakland, California, when the subject of finding guitars arose. I asked Serge if it would be possible to create a computer program to automatically call people on the telephone with a prerecorded message asking if they had any vintage guitars to sell.

"Yes!" Serge yapped. I told him that he looked like a hunting dog that had just found a pheasant. He said, "That's it! We'll call it the Bird Dog."

The next day Serge had completed the interface for the new device. It depicted a bird dog crossing the computer screen and then freezing on point before the words "BIRD DOG" in huge script materialized.

Serge set up the Bird Dog to call every number in a given area code . . . every single solitary number. And those who answered their phones were greeted with this simple and happy prerecorded proposition:

> *(Opening riff to Freddie King's famous blues song "Hideaway")*
>
> Hello, my name is Michael. I am calling you today looking for some old guitars. I am especially looking for old Gibson, Fender, Martin, and Gretsch guitars that were made between 1940 and 1970.
>
> *(Follow-up riff to Freddie King's "Hideaway")*
>
> If you have any old guitars, please press 1 now.
>
> If you don't have any old guitars, but know someone who does, please press 2 now.

The Bird Dog was also programmed to detect an answering machine or voice mail picking up, and it would leave a message for any potential guitar owner. If we got a "hit," the program would ask what make and model of guitar the person had, what year it had been built, and so on. At the end of the day, without having left the house, we could sift through the American homeland in search of beloved and valuable vintage instruments! We could add tens of thousands of guitars to our database with important details such as make, model, and the year of manufacture. It seemed as if we had a possible gold mine search computer on our hands.

We continued to refine the program. Before we launched Bird Dog, we decided to expand the mission. Why not ask folks whether they had any other collectibles? We decided to query the public regarding any Rolex watches that they might like to sell. An old Ferrari in the barn, perhaps? At the end of the day, we speculated, we could effectively inventory the contents of every residence in the United States and become a broker or trading house of any and all merchandise that had resale value.

The Bird Dog's first foray was a short, local, trial run. Although the test was a success, a number of technical bugs had to be addressed. Serge went back to work. Finally, just a few days later, it was time for the full-scale launch. Ironically, the huge search potential of Bird Dog existed in one normal-size personal computer. We set up the Dog in a spare back bedroom at my house and turned it loose. Serge and I were like a couple of devious kids who had just concocted a dangerous experiment in our high school chemistry class. I remember vividly as we nervously pushed the start button—and heard a quiet whirring from our Promethean pooch. One after another, Bird Dog called each local telephone number in sequence.

Meanwhile, we were concerned that people would be wary of responding to the Dog's entreaties, because they would be giving away private data about their possessions and valuables. Would the public be apprehensive of this new telemarketing apparatus? What if they considered it a scam—or a way for some enterprising thief to case their houses? All we could do was wait and see.

We got a number of positive responses straightaway. We gave people a choice of replying to the Bird Dog directly by entering a response on the telephone keypad or calling our toll-free telephone number to speak to us directly. Quickly we began to get calls on very desirable instruments as well as other collectibles that we could buy and sell at a profit. The Bird Dog was a success, and Serge and I determined to scale it to the highest level of economic performance. We envisioned buying vintage cars, guitars, watches, fine art, jewelry, real property—it was all fruitful and fair game. However, we were to soon learn that the Dog had a few fleas.

One evening, a storm caused a power outage, stopping the Dog from hunting at approximately seven o'clock in the evening. When the power finally came back on, the Dawg resumed his search, but by then it was three in the morning, which resulted in, shall we say, a few disgruntled respondents. I suspect that the five thousand or so people the pup awoke that morning would rather have had another few hours of shut-eye. Sadly, because of this unfortunate episode, we had no choice but to euthanize the pooch. He was given a proper burial and Serge performed a rousing eulogy. Cicero himself would have been proud.

Since we'd decided to let sleeping dogs lie, I was glad I still had my aptitude to connect with the people who responded to my ads. My acquired knowledge of guitar manufacture, history, rarity, and other factors that add up to a guitar's true value were indispensable assets. Notwithstanding the somber burial of the Bird Dog, new discoveries kept appearing. As such, there are some old stories that still need to be told.

One noteworthy event occurred in 1981: I saw an ad in the *Richmond Independent* newspaper for a Fender Telecaster guitar priced at $200. I called the number and asked if the Telecaster was an older model. The seller, a man named Dave, said, "No, it's a new one, and it's a really good one!" *Too bad*, I thought, and asked about the color of the pickguard, hoping against hope that he was wrong and that it was an older model. "Black," he said, "and the guitar is kind of mustard yellow. It just says 'Fender' on it, but I know it's a Telecaster."

I knew right away what that meant. It was likely not a Telecaster but rather a rare 1950 Fender "Nocaster" guitar. So I jumped in my Volkswagen and drove as fast as I could to this fellow's apartment in nearby San Pablo. On the way, my car developed a severe problem with its axle. Long story short, my car was hamstrung and I was forced to drive at an embarrassing fifteen miles per hour to see this guitar. Yet soon a beautiful 1950 Fender "Nocaster" was mine for $200.

The "Nocaster" was in essence a Fender Broadcaster, the first electric Spanish-style guitar manufactured by Fender— and one of the most rare and collectible Fender guitars ever produced. About eight months after the Broadcaster was introduced in early 1950, Fender was sued by the Gretsch drum company, which had a drum they called the Broadcaster. It took Fender a few months to rename the guitar the Telecaster and to print headstock decals to match. So, in the meantime, they clipped the old "Fender Broadcaster" decals at the factory and applied them to instruments now identified simply as "Fender." Collectors came to call this interim model the "Nocaster"—not a Broadcaster, but not quite yet a Telecaster. That rare guitar I bought for $200 is worth $50,000 in today's market.

Another time I had a call from a woman in a little town in Arizona called Lake Havasu. Hers was a very sad story. The woman's sister had purchased a Fender guitar brand new in 1951 for $250, a sizeable amount of money back then. She had owned it for only two weeks before she was killed in a car accident. The guitar was placed under a bed and stayed there until 1996. When I opened the guitar's case, the latches were stiff from lack of use. Inside was a pristine, unused 1951 "Nocaster"— one of the most beautiful, and beautiful-sounding, guitars ever made. The instrument was worth substantially more than the $5,000 I planned to offer. I could have ended up paying $10,000 to $12,000 if some other dealer had been bidding on it at that time. But I thought if I offered the woman and her husband— nice folks who were probably in their seventies—the $10,000 I would have gladly paid, she would get scared and balk at selling. That sort of thing happened to me over and over. I could sense that her husband was gun shy and didn't want her to sell it at all, but she seemed to want to let it go. I offered the $5,000, and the owner jumped at it. When I walked out the door with it she said, "I'm glad that someone got it who appreciates it. It probably would have been sold at a garage sale after we died." I loved that guitar.

Another desert call brought me to an amazing 1955 Stratocaster. A chap named Quentin Daly, who lived north of Palm Springs way out in the high desert, claimed he had a '55 Stratocaster for sale. He lived down a long dirt road, out in the middle of nowhere. When I arrived at his large California Ranch–style home, I could see that Quentin had money. He had a very expensive motor home sitting on the side of the house. His lawn was beautifully coiffed and his hedges were manicured better than Paris Hilton's toes. I rang the doorbell and was greeted by a tanned Jack LaLanne look-alike in a tan jumpsuit. After the perfunctory small talk, Quentin pulled out what appeared to be a virtually unplayed sunburst 1955 Strat, though it had one glaring problem: it appeared that the paint along the edge of the guitar had been refinished many years ago. So I offered Quentin $4,000—though I would have paid closer to 10K if that beautiful guitar had not been modified. Old Quentin scratched his chin for what seemed to be fifteen minutes before politely declining my offer. He wanted six grand. I passed on the guitar. As I drove out on that long dirt road, a flock of crows followed my van and squawked at me very loudly. I think they were trying to tell me that I had made a grievous error by not buying that instrument.

A couple of years later I was in that same high desert area and called upon old Quentin. Prices had gone up substantially in those two years and I was ready now to pay the $6,000 or perhaps more, notwithstanding the "issue" the guitar had. This time when I arrived and asked Quentin what price he was prepared to accept for the guitar, he said he would take my earlier, $4,000 offer. To sweeten up the deal, Quentin also offered to throw in several other rarities, including an old Fender tweed amplifier and some vintage catalogs. So I bought the entire lot.

When I got home I consulted with a friend who inspected this Stratocaster; he suggested that it might just be an odd but original paint job, and not refinished on the sides. I quickly took the guitar and conducted a forensic examination under a black light. A black light allows the detection of substances that exhibit a fluorescent effect, such as different layers of paint or lacquer from different periods of time. Black light testing is commonly used to authenticate other antiques and banknotes. In short, it allows you to see if paint or lacquer has been added over time. After performing a detailed analysis, that convinced me that the guitar did indeed have the original finish, I did a dance that would have made Fred Astaire envious. The guitar was worth about $18,000, and with the amp, over $20,000. Not a bad day's work, especially when I'd been so doubtful about the instrument's value. I sent Mr. Daly a nice check to compensate for the difference. But old Quentin sent the check back uncashed and thanked me. "A deal's a deal, son. Enjoy the guitar."

7

WILLARD "FLEETWOOD" BROUGHAM

On a warm summer day I received a phone message from one Willard Brougham in Vallejo, California, just north of San Francisco near the Napa Valley wine country. I remember the exact date: June 17, 1994. This was the day O.J. Simpson led the infamous slow-speed chase down the 405 freeway in Los Angeles before his arrest on double murder charges in the "crime of the century." I remember this vividly because I was on that same L.A. freeway, on my way to yet another guitar deal, and listening to live coverage on the radio, glued to the unfolding events like most of the rest of the nation.

"They're headed north on the 405 freeway," said the breathless announcer.

"Hey wait," I said out loud, "I'm on the 405 freeway too!"

"They're coming up near Sunset Boulevard," the coverage continued, and I realized I was also near Sunset. So I sped to the next exit and pulled off in hope of getting a view of the fugitive and the media circus—and sure enough, a battery of cop cars, reporters, news helicopters, and one white Ford Bronco passed right by me. For that minute, I was an eyewitness to a sad history.

When I returned to my hotel, there was the message from

Mr. Brougham waiting for me: "My name is Willard, and I got here a 1958 Gibson Les Paul geetar. Call me, will ya'?"

Could this be a Sunburst Les Paul? I was always on the lookout for this legendary guitar but did not want to appear overanxious. So I decided to wait a couple of days to return the call. I'd learned from long experience that if you show too much enthusiasm, a seller can get cold feet.

"Yeah, I got it," Willard Brougham assured me when I rang back a week later. "It's a 1958 Gibson Les Paul, all right. I just had it appraised for $16,000. Can you spend that much on a guitar?"

"Well," I replied cagily, "that depends. I'd really need to see it first." I was wondering whether the guitar had really been appraised. If it was the coveted Sunburst model Les Paul Standard, it was worth much more than $16,000. But if the top of the guitar had the solid gold finish (called a "gold top"), then that price would be just about retail.

"Is it a sunburst top?" was my next question.

"What is that?" he asked.

"Is the face of the guitar a red color around the edge that fades to yellow?"

"No," the voice on the other end replied. "It's just yellow."

"You mean just one color—a solid gold color?" I persisted.

"Yeah," came the answer. "It's a solid gold."

"Fair enough," I said. "We're dealing with a 1958 Goldtop here." Now, a 1958 Les Paul Standard, known as a Goldtop, was a valuable guitar in its own right. The Goldtop was exactly the same guitar as the coveted Sunburst model, except that the maple top of the Goldtop was painted solid gold, whereas the sunburst top featured a translucent, two-toned finish called "sunburst" by the Gibson company. The Goldtop was coveted—but was not nearly as sought-after as the legendary Sunburst. I told Willard I still wanted to come over and see it—to which he agreed, but he told me he was busy that week, so I should try later: "Call me in a couple a' weeks." It was his turn to play hard to get. I kept in contact with Willard and he finally invited me over to take a gander.

Willard's decidedly down-market home, in a lower-class neighborhood without the slightest "curb appeal," led me to believe he would love to end the day with $16,000 in his pocket. Real estate is a trusty litmus test I use to predict my likelihood of success in buying guitars. If a seller's house is in a nice neighborhood but looks run-down, I predict a much better chance of scoring the instrument. If the house is in a less affluent neighborhood but is well kept, my odds diminish. It follows that if the home is in an upper-class neighborhood and well kept, my chances drop precipitously. As I pulled up to Willard's home, I felt pretty good about my prospects. This is just experience speaking on this point.

I knocked and a black gentleman, perhaps sixty-five years old, opened the door. "Willard?" I asked, as he quickly sized me up.

"You can call me Fleetwood . . . Fleetwood Brougham."

"Fleetwood" was a wiry fellow, sporting a gold front tooth, a watered-down southern drawl, and the unmistakable scent of wave pomade. I was invited in and we sat down at the kitchen table. His wife, a younger Filipina woman, provided a tasty beverage. We chatted for half an hour before he went to his bedroom. It was there that he had stored his guitar in a closet since 1960, when he had won it in a poker game.

Fleetwood returned with a bundle in a blanket. As he unwrapped it, I caught a glimpse of the guitar's headstock and concluded that it might be a Les Paul Junior, or perhaps another much less valuable model that had been marketed in the fifties. This just goes to show how wrong even an "expert" can be.

When he finally unveiled the instrument, I feasted my eyes on a genuine 1958 Sunburst Les Paul, with its absolutely stunning trademark curly maple wood grain—or "flame," as we call it in the collecting world. Here was a guitar hunter's dream come true. Mr. Brougham's guitar was better than anything in my collection, nicer even than another 1958 Sunburst I owned and had prized for years. It was truly a once-in-a-lifetime find, with no scratches or any other damage that vintage guitars often sustain. I had to keep my hands from shaking as I inspected this glorious guitar. I cannot begin to describe the excitement I felt at this discovery. It would not be an overstatement to say that I was desperate to own it.

"What are your plans with this guitar?" I managed to ask. "Are you prepared to sell it?"

"Yeah," he allowed. "I might. If I can get the right price."

The operative word in his reply was "might." I knew only too well what that meant. "Might" just as easily could mean "might not." I also knew that, in the current market, the Sunburst was worth a cool $60,000 in Japan.

He had mentioned an appraisal of $16,000 on the phone, but rather than offering that sum immediately, I replied with my own qualifier, saying, "I'm interested and might buy it." The game was on. If I made an offer too quickly he would likely shop his treasure to every music store in the world to see if he could get a higher offer. I had been through that song and dance one too many times. Though I had the cash in my pocket and was determined to go home with the guitar, I was playing this one very conservatively. It would take just one other knowledgeable dealer to raise the ante to $20,000 or $30,000. If that happened I would still buy it, but I'd be forced to resell it. I wanted more than anything to add that guitar to my collection, and I could only do that if the price was modest.

"Let's both think about it for a few days," I suggested, and Willard agreed with a clap of his hands. I could tell he was disappointed that I hadn't agreed to the $16,000 without hesitation. My strategy was simple but risky: I was willing to wait rather than drive up the price by seeming too eager—even though there was a possibility some other dealer might beat me to that jewel.

As Fleetwood walked me out to my car, he confided that he had recently lost his driver's license due to a DUI arrest. "Yeah, I can't drive anywhere," he said, "and I can't work 'cause my business is rotor tilling and I can't haul equipment no more." I remember being impressed that this old guy was spry enough to handle a rotor tiller.

"Well," I replied, "I know some people who might need your services if you want some work," adding I had a small cargo van I might be able to put at his disposal.

Fleetwood flashed a wide, gold-toothed grin. "I might just take ya' up on that." When, a few days later, Fleetwood called asking for a ride, a friendship was forged. He was a nice man. As happy as I was to oblige him, I always had that Sunburst gleaming in the back of my mind; I had lost more than a little sleep worrying that I would not ultimately be able to lay my hands on that beauty.

The circus went on for months, with Fleetwood calling every few days, asking me to chauffeur him here and there. Finally, after I prodded him about his decision, he relented. "Well, Cool Breeze," he mused, "I think I'm going to sell you my guitar, but you got to throw in another one so I have a little somethin' to play."

I scurried down to the friendly neighborhood Guitar Center and picked up a brand new "reissue" of the Sunburst, basically a modern version that looked just like Fleetwood's original 1958 model. Despite the similarity, Fleetwood spurned the substitute, so I had to return the guitar and replace it with a Gibson L6S that he finally approved of. He was a finicky old fellow, and quite clever. He knew he had me over a barrel. After a few more trips squiring him around town, I insisted he give an answer: would he sell the guitar to me for $16,000 or not?

"Well," he replied, scratching his head, "If I sell you that guitar I want to sell that scooter along with it." It was a genteel form of blackmail: if I wanted the Les Paul, I had to take the broken-down old motorbike in his garage for an additional $1,500. By this time Fleetwood obviously knew I really wanted his guitar and he was starting to squeeze me accordingly. I acquiesced, making the best of the situation by agreeing that I had always wanted a scooter.

We finally had a deal . . . or so I thought. "Fleetwood, wrap up that guitar and the scooter," I said when I called him on the phone to seal the deal. "I'm coming over to get them."

But once more he slipped through my fingers. "Not today," he replied. "I want to do some work on the scooter first. I'll call you in a week or two." He was driving me insane, and I think he was quite enjoying it.

After what seemed an eternity—actually only a few days— Fleetwood got back to me. "Come on over," he said. "I'm ready for ya'. And bring cash."

I scurried over to his house. But instead of Fleetwood, his wife greeted me at the door. I had long ago surmised that Fleetwood's spouse was a "mail-order bride." She had always been in the background, but now she injected herself directly into our negotiations.

"You know," she said with a sly smile, "I have a daughter back in the Philippines and she wants to get married. If you really want this guitar maybe she comes as part of the deal. You can be my son-in-law."

"You've got to be kidding," I mumbled. "Now I have to get married to get my hands on this damn thing?" But the wheels were already in motion, with Fleetwood's wife making a long-distance phone call and putting me on the phone with her daughter.

"What do you do for a living?" my prospective bride inquired, although I suspect she fully knew I was about to drop sixteen large on her stepfather's guitar. We chatted breezily for a few minutes and I was beginning to wonder whether this might not be such a bad arrangement after all; she seemed quite nice. Then it occurred to me that if her mother actually had to arrange a marriage for her, she was probably, to use the old saying, nothing to write home about. And of course, that old song by Jimmy Soul came into my head: *"If you want to be happy for the rest of your life, never make a pretty woman your wife."*

But Fleetwood's wife must have been a mind reader because, unprompted, she blurted out, "My daughter is very beautiful."

"Sure," I told myself, "that's what they all say." This made it even more surprising when she pulled out a photograph of a gorgeous, brown-skinned bombshell with dark hair and sparkling eyes. "Damn . . ." I thought, "here I am, spending my youth running around the planet looking for old guitars. I have no social life, no girlfriend, and no prospects for either one. Maybe this is my lucky day. I could walk away with a beautiful girl, my dream guitar, and a scooter thrown in for laughs!"

Well, it didn't quite work out that way. Fleetwood did sell me the Les Paul that day, but although I did have a few more conversations with the lovely lady from the Philippines, she eventually married someone else (most likely a trombone dealer). I gave the scooter to a friend.

"I will never sell this guitar," I declared after I brought that Sunburst home. It was one of the finest guitars I ever came across. An amazing find, in brand-new condition, it played perfectly and sounded divine. As it turned out, however, I did sell it just three years later, along with the rest of my collection, including two 1958 Gibson Explorers and another 1958 Les Paul. I sacrificed these instruments to buy an expensive home.

Part of me really wanted to settle down, to get off the road once and for all. Of course, I dearly miss those guitars, but most of all I miss the Sunburst Les Paul I bought from Willard "Fleetwood" Brougham. It was a very special instrument, the culmination of the treasure hunter's dream come true—and a reminder of the trophy bride that got away.

8

HOLIER THAN THOU

Over the years I followed many leads, real and otherwise, in my hunt for rare and famous guitars. There have been many stories of guitars simply owned or played by a famous musician that have become supremely expensive. The Stratocaster played at Woodstock by Jimi Hendrix is a good example. Without its history with Jimi, this guitar would be worth perhaps $10,000. But Jimi's historic Woodstock guitar sold for a reported $1 million in 1992.

Without a storied lineage, guitars have limited intrinsic worth, but certain instruments have become incredibly valuable simply because of their pedigree. Another example is the Hofner Bass guitar Paul McCartney has used since the early 1960s. Sir Paul's inexpensive Hofner might well be the most valuable musical instrument in the history of the world. If this instrument had not become the bass guitar of choice for the Beatle, it would likely be just another bass guitar sitting on a rack in a music store somewhere collecting dust.

The rumor mill consistently produces chatter about celebrity-owned instruments, but reports of one of these instruments always stood out to me because the storied guitar that I refer to was rumored to be both a masterpiece of guitar craftsmanship and made specifically for a guitar legend. One big problem existed with this guitar: nobody knew of its whereabouts.

Guitar collector and journalist Robb Lawrence, perhaps best known for his Rare Bird column in *Guitar Player* magazine, told me a story many years ago about a one-of-a-kind rosewood Stratocaster that had been custom-made for Jimi Hendrix. If this instrument truly existed, it would be one of the most valuable guitars ever made by the hand of man.

A few years after hearing about this legendary guitar I received a telephone call responding to an advertisement I had placed in the *Los Angeles Times*. "I've got five guitars," the caller said, "and I'm willing to part with them if the price is right." His name was James "Jim" Wilkoski and he was an attorney in the Los Angeles area. Among the instruments he described to me, one sent my pulse racing. "I've got an all-rosewood Stratocaster from 1968—but I want a lot of money for it."

I replied, "You've got my attention, Jim."

My first thought was what any knowledgeable Fender aficionado would ask upon hearing that description: "Could this be the long-lost Jimi Hendrix Stratocaster?" I asked Jim for more details on the guitar. He claimed it was in pristine condition and, since it had been previously owned by a top executive at Fender, it had never been put on the market.

"I represented the Fender executive in his divorce. This is what he gave me in barter for my services," Jim explained. I asked a few more pointed questions, but it was obvious to both of us that I needed to come down and take a look at it. He suggested I grab a shuttle the next day, but there was one question that would not wait.

"How much money do you want for it?" I asked.

"Fourteen thousand dollars," he calmly replied.

"Wow," I exclaimed. "That's a big number." But I knew that if it *was* the Hendrix guitar, it would be worth every penny and more—perhaps a lot more. So, the next morning, as Steve Miller would say, I hopped on a "big ol' jet airliner" and flew down to Los Angeles.

When I got to Los Angeles, I met James Wilkoski at his law office. Jim looked a bit like Willie Nelson, sans ponytail, dressed in business attire. He was spot-on about the guitar's condition. It could have been sold as new. More importantly, the guitar possessed every last detail required of the guitar custom-made for Jimi Hendrix.

"Do you know the history of this instrument?" I asked.

It had been made for a famous musician, Jim told me, before becoming the property of the former director of marketing at Fender. This, too, was right in line with the story I had heard about the Hendrix rosewood Stratocaster. At any rate, it was worth $14,000 even if it was *not* the legendary Hendrix custom guitar, so I agreed to his price. Only then did I realize I did not have enough money with me. I would have to come back a few days later to conclude the deal. Naturally, by the time I came back, Wilkoski started having second thoughts. I kicked myself for not carrying enough good U.S. currency to buy the guitar outright, and I suspected he was questioning my willingness to agree to his steep price so quickly.

"What are you going to do with this guitar?" he asked sharply when I arrived at his law office the second time. It was clear from his queries that he wanted to find out exactly what I knew about the instrument. When I only supplied vague answers, trying to sidestep the possibility that it could be a one-of-a-kind guitar, he abruptly tried to back out of the deal. I insisted that I was not going back to San Francisco without that Strat and showed him the binding legal contract written down in black and white—with his John Hancock prominently affixed to the agreement.

Jim was surprised that I had such a formidable grasp of contract law. He said he "might" abide by the deal with one notable condition: he wanted first right of refusal if I ever decided to sell the guitar. It was no problem for me to have a buyer in my back pocket, so I agreed. He looked at me through squinty eyes. "Deal." We shook hands (for the second time), the remaining money was counted out, and I headed back to San Francisco believing that I had scored the best instrument of my career.

The guitar was magnificent in every way; both the body and the neck were made entirely of rosewood. I knew Fender had made a rosewood Telecaster played by former Beatle George Harrison, but I had never seen such construction in a Stratocaster. Intrigued, I started doing research. I decided to call Robb Lawrence to see what else he could tell me about the mythical guitar that he had mentioned years before. I had no idea that this was the opening salvo in an investigation that would, as far as the guitar world was concerned, rival the debate over the Shroud of Turin in its intensity and passion. I put on my investigator's cap, lit up a pipe, and grabbed a trusty magnifying glass. It was time for some good old-fashioned private eye work.

When I phoned Mr. Lawrence he said, "I know one of the guys who helped make those custom rosewood guitars. He was an apprentice at Fender. His name is Phil Kubicki and he lives in Santa Barbara." Phil, he continued, had left Fender in the early 1970s to start a company that made high-quality custom bass guitars.

"Let's go see him," I said enthusiastically.

The next day I met Robb in Malibu and we drove up the Pacific Coast Highway to visit Kubicki. We arrived at Phil's guitar shop, down a side street in scenic Santa Barbara, on a bright and beautiful Southern California day. Phil, a gracious host with a wealth of inside information on guitar lore, took a quick look at the rosewood Stratocaster. That was all he needed, or so it seemed.

"Yeah, this looks like it," he remarked and proceeded to tell us how he had worked in the late 1960s and early 1970s as an apprentice to Roger Rossmeisl, the head of Fender's research and development department. The Fender marketing department wanted the company to produce two special guitars: one to present to Hendrix and one for George Harrison. Each of these artists had done much to spread the renown of the Fender Company by using their guitars. Hendrix, especially, had sent sales of Stratocasters into the stratosphere (excuse the pun) during his short but illustrious career. The company was hoping to get the same sort of implied endorsement from Harrison by giving him a unique instrument to play, one built especially for him.

To accomplish this, the Fender craftsmen built an all-rosewood Telecaster for the Beatles' pioneering lead guitarist and an all-rosewood Stratocaster for Hendrix. Once the instruments were presented to the artists, the plan was to put the two new rosewood models into regular production.

Phil also told us something not generally known, even by the most knowledgeable guitar experts: Fender had produced *two* of the presentation Stratocasters, intending that the higher-quality of the two instruments would be presented to Jimi. This raised an interesting question, and a potential problem in establishing the provenance and value of the guitar I had bought from James Wilkoski: since there were *two* rosewood Stratocasters and they were more or less identical, how could I tell which of the two I had?

Following his fascinating narrative, Phil offered to take the guitar apart to try to determine which of the two Strats I had.

On closer examination, he believed my instrument was *not* the one chosen for Hendrix. First, he pointed out, there was some wood filler on the back of the guitar.

"We would never have used wood filler on such an important instrument," he insisted. "And there's a little piece of tape inside the body that gives the formula for the finish on the guitar. It's not likely that we would have left that on a presentation guitar.

"I'm not sure," he concluded, "I could be wrong, but I'm inclined to believe this would be the other one—the one not chosen as a presentation model for Mr. Hendrix."

Rats! But I was not finished with my investigation, not by a long shot. I called Tom Wheeler at *Guitar Player* magazine and told him about the guitar and Kubicki's inspection and evaluation. Tom asked if I could provide a photo for the magazine's Encore column. There he wrote an article recounting the story and Phil's conclusion: that, in all probability, the instrument I had was not the guitar destined for Jimi Hendrix.

Despite Phil's opinion, I remained skeptical on the subject of that rosewood Stratocaster. But then, who was I to argue with a man who had been there at the inception? Surprisingly, a few years later, Kubicki wrote an article in *Vintage Guitar* magazine about the Hendrix Stratocaster and the Harrison Telecaster. And in this article, he directly contradicted what he had told us that day in Santa Barbara. *Huh?*

The first glaring inconsistency in the article was that Kubicki now claimed he *had* used wood filler on the presentation guitars. He even singled out the brand name of the filler. He also revealed in great detail how Fender had made a unique triple-layer pickguard that alternated black on white on black. He asserted that three pickguards had been made for the two Stratocasters, with a spare as a replacement.

When we visited Phil, he still had the extra pickguard in his shop and showed it to us. He compared the spare pickguard with the one on my guitar, and they matched precisely—but they had two layers, not the three he later described in the article.

My doubts about Phil's power of recollection began to be confirmed. Mind you, this was some thirty-five years after Phil had first helped to make these guitars. Remembering the minute details that were at issue here, in my opinion, was far beyond the recall of most people. I believe that Phil was completely honest and forthright with me. It was just so very long removed from the present that a forensic analysis of the instrument was going to prove much more reliable than the frailty of human memory.

Mr. Kubicki concluded his article in *Vintage Guitar* by describing how, after Hendrix's death, the front office had called for the presentation Stratocaster. He remembered personally delivering it to the receptionist for safekeeping. "That was the last time I saw the Jimi guitar," he wrote, inadvertently providing an important clue.

A month after that article appeared, *Vintage Guitar* printed a letter that had been sent to the editor shedding significant new light on the fate of the Hendrix Strat. The letter, by former Fender employee Cheri Newton, described how she had come upon an all-rosewood Stratocaster in an outbuilding at Fender headquarters in the mid-1970s. She asked her boss if she could display the magnificent instrument in her office and was given permission. She subsequently loaned the guitar out to a friend, and it was never returned.

I put on my thinking cap after reading the letter. There were only two rosewood Stratocasters made in 1968. One was hand-delivered by Phil Kubicki to Fender's front office in September of 1970. Another was found in an outbuilding in or around 1973. I knew that the guitar that had gone to the front office was the one intended for Hendrix. Thus all I had to do in order to establish that I had the Hendrix guitar was confirm my guitar was the one that had been delivered to the front office.

I tried to call Mr. Wilkoski, the attorney who had sold me the guitar, but I could not make contact with him. Next, I telephoned the California Bar Association, and they informed me that Mr. Wilkoski was no longer practicing law in California. They had no contact information for him. Ringo Starr was right when he said, "It don't come easy."

So I decided to undertake a thorough search of my notes from the purchase of the guitar; it has long been my habit to take extensive notes about an important instrument's history. In my notes I found the names of two Fender executives directly associated with the guitar: Dave Gupton and Roger Garvin. I started asking any and everybody how I could find Gupton or Garvin. Robb Lawrence, who remembered Roger Garvin but didn't know his whereabouts, obligingly called longtime Fender executive George Fullerton, who remembered Gupton but had long since lost touch with him.

The break came when another friend who had worked at Fender in the 1970s told me Mr. Garvin was alive and well and living in Las Vegas. I did a property search and found his address, but his phone was unlisted. All I could do was to write him a letter at the listed address.

Several anxious weeks passed before I got a call from the elusive Roger Garvin, former Fender executive. He proved very helpful. He immediately remembered the custom rosewood guitars made for Hendrix and Harrison and told me the rosewood Telecasters had been put into production, then dropped because of manufacturing difficulties. Garvin's knowledge ended there and he professed not to know the fate of the Hendrix rosewood Stratocaster. Before I hung up, I asked if he knew

Dave Gupton—a variation on my old habit of asking potential sellers if they knew of other guitars on the market.

"Sure, I know Dave," he replied. "He was the director of marketing for Fender. In fact, he might have been the one who ultimately ended up with that rosewood Stratocaster."

I had one last question for him. "Where at Fender was Dave Gupton's office located?"

"In the front office," he replied.

With this additional tidbit, I was making real progress. I now had the name of the guitar's most likely recipient, the chief marketing exec who had worked in the Fender front office where the Hendrix guitar had been delivered. The next challenge was to find Dave Gupton and verify all of this. I launched an Internet hunt, did property searches, and even sent correspondence to a Dave Gupton I found in Los Angeles. Unfortunately, it was the wrong guy and the letter was returned. Finally, I called George Fullerton to see if he could help me find Gupton. He remembered Dave, but had not seen him since 1970. The contact was far from fruitless, however. Fullerton recalled another ex-Fender employee, Bill Carson of Nashville, who had been friends with Gupton and might have stayed in touch with him.

"I know Dave Gupton pretty well," Carson told me when I reached him by telephone. "The last time I heard, he was in Reno. That was three years ago, but as far as I know, he's still alive and kicking." Property searches in Reno yielded my next clue: an address for a Dave Gupton, again without a phone number. I sent yet another letter requesting, if he was the same Dave Gupton who had once worked at the Fender Musical Instruments Corporation, that he please get in touch with me.

A few weeks later the call came, with the name Dave Gupton on my caller I.D. Bingo! I took out my notepad in hopes that I could at last solve the mystery of the twin rosewood Stratocasters. I was starting to understand how Sam Spade might have felt as he was on the hunt for the Maltese Falcon.

After introducing myself and telling Dave of my wide-ranging inquiry, I asked him the critical question. "Did you happen to own a Fender Stratocaster that was made out of rosewood?"

"I certainly did," he replied.

"Can you tell me how it came into your possession?" I asked.

Forty-five minutes later he had given me the whole story. He was gracious and cordial.

"I think that guitar was made for Billy Gibbons from ZZ Top," he ventured as he tried to jog his memory.

"I've been told it was made for Jimi Hendrix," I replied, hoping I was not barking up the wrong tree.

"Maybe it was Jimi Hendrix," he said. "Just maybe it was." After thinking about it for a moment he said, "We made more than a few custom-built guitars in those days. It was surely a noteworthy musician; that's why we were building them in the first place. With those rosewood Strats, as I remember, we made a couple of special presentation guitars and I ended up with one."

"Well," I asked, "when did you get the guitar?" It was a crucial question that would establish the timeline.

"I had it in 1970," he replied; "then years later I had to give it up in trade to the attorney who handled my divorce." The final piece of the puzzle fell into place. Since the second Strat had been found three years later in an outbuilding at the Fender factory and Gupton recalled having his guitar in the Fender front office in 1970, in my mind I had conclusive proof that I owned the real Hendrix rosewood Stratocaster.

"Can you write me a letter detailing what you told me today?" I asked. He immediately agreed. The next day, I forwarded Dave all my information on the guitar, including the Kubicki article in *Vintage Guitar*, the letter from Cheri Newton in *Vintage*

Guitar, a sheaf of press clippings, and my own letter stating the important provenance of the Strat. Then I sat back to wait for the final written authentication.

Six months later I was still waiting. When day after day nothing showed up in the mailbox, I finally called Gupton back, kindly reminding him that he was going to verify in writing his account of the rosewood Strat.

"I can't remember anything about the guitar," Dave replied with an evasiveness that stunned me.

"Huh? What do you mean you can't remember?" I replied, totally taken aback and, I'm afraid, losing my cool for a moment. "Did you get a knock on the head that gave you amnesia? We had a long and detailed discussion about it."

"Sorry . . ." he replied blandly. "Like I told you, I don't know anything about it. My memory is very fuzzy these days. Can't help you." More than anything, it sounded like he just wanted to get off the phone.

I took a deep breath. "Now, wait a minute," I beseeched him. "You told me that you owned this guitar at one time and that you traded for services to an attorney, James Wilkoski. Is that not correct, sir?"

"Well, yes, I guess so," he muttered hesitantly.

It was at that point that a light went on in my head. Since I had last spoken to the retired Fender executive, he had apparently learned about the controversy surrounding the guitar and decided to keep a low profile. I speculated that Gupton was now fearful he was going to be part of a story he didn't want to be involved with. Why else would he have gone from being completely helpful to being utterly unwilling to talk? Whatever the reason, it was clear he had comprehensively clammed up.

I blamed myself, in part, for the situation and regretted sending him the articles and background materials detailing the

Strat's now very public history. All things considered, it would have been wiser to let him think I was just a curious collector and keep any hint of possible big money out of the discussion.

I made one last effort to get him to cooperate, recounting that he had told me he thought the guitar was made for ZZ Top's Billy Gibbons and that it had come into his possession in 1970 from the front office at Fender. "You said you were going to write me a letter," I repeated, "and now you're telling me you don't remember any of this?"

"That's right," he replied stiffly. "I don't know, and I don't want to talk about it anymore." To emphasize his point, he hung up, leaving me with a loud dial tone droning in my ear.

This appeared to be a major setback in my efforts to document the guitar's provenance. But I was not about to give up, not after all the time and effort that I had put into proving the bona fides of that guitar. A few months after that disheartening phone call, I sent one of my confidants, Dave Precheur, to personally visit Dave Gupton at home in Reno. His instructions were to explain the whole matter again and respectfully ask Gupton to sign the letter of authentication as he had agreed. At the same time Gupton was to be reassured I would use the information only to establish the provenance of the rosewood Stratocaster to the next buyer.

When Dave Precheur knocked at the Gupton residence, Gupton's wife answered and said her husband was not at home. Precheur patiently explained to her what we needed and what was required to certify the guitar was indeed the Hendrix rosewood Strat.

"Mr. Gupton only has to verify that it was created especially for someone famous, as he told Michael it was, and that he had the guitar in 1970 and possessed it until he exchanged it for the services of his attorney, James Wilkoski. It is a simple matter of that documentation, and these facts are precisely what your husband told Michael about the guitar on the phone."

Precheur repeated this pitch all over again when Dave Gupton himself finally came home. "All right, all right," said the exasperated former guitar executive. "I'll do it. I'll even write the letter myself." Precheur returned triumphant, but my good feeling did not last. Three more months passed with no letter from Gupton.

I was beginning to take this contest of wills personally. I finally sent an employee, Kermit Goodman, to visit Mr. Gupton, equipping him with a draft of the proposed letter on a laptop computer with a printer. That way, Gupton would have no excuse to avoid delivering what he had twice promised. Still, we were prepared for any excuse he might dream up. But this time Gupton did not bother with excuses; he simply dug in his heels.

"No, I'm not going to sign it," he told Kermit, clearly annoyed that he was still being hounded.

In response, Kermit called me and put Gupton on the phone. "Hi, Dave, I'm back," I said, equally put out. "You told me you would sign this letter. Twice now! What in tarnation is going on?"

"I'm not going to be pressured like this," he shot back.

"Dave, this is important," I insisted. Once again, I read him my notes from the first day I had talked to him on the phone. Gupton was getting more exasperated by the minute, but by that time I think he realized I was not going to give up, no matter what.

"Look," he said after a long pause. "All I'm saying is that I had the guitar in 1970 and that I bartered it to my lawyer."

"That's all I need, Dave," I assured him. "That would be enough to fully document the guitar."

"Fine," he replied, "but I'm not signing anything right now."

You vile owl! I thought to myself, but swallowed hard and tried to stay focused. "How about tomorrow morning?" I asked. "I'll have Kermit come back and type the letter according to your specifications. You don't have to do anything else. You can make your statement any way you want, as long as you sign it."

"No," he replied adamantly, "I'm going to write it and send it myself."

I had heard that before, but there was nothing I could do. We seemed to have reached an impasse. There was no chance, I assumed, that Gupton would follow through and write the long-promised letter, but lo and behold, two weeks later I got a signed document with exactly the wording needed: that he had received the guitar in 1970 when he was director of marketing at Fender and had later traded it to his lawyer, James Wilkoski.

The letter was a critical piece of corroborating evidence, because it documented that Dave Gupton had owned the guitar and had possession of the instrument before the other rosewood Stratocaster had been found in an outbuilding at the Fender facility. More importantly, Gupton had taken possession of the guitar in 1970 while at the Fender front office—the same office where Phil Kubicki remembered delivering it.

To this day I don't know why Dave Gupton was so reluctant to admit the part he'd played in the saga of the Hendrix Strat. Perhaps he tasted sour grapes after learning the guitar he had bartered away had become very valuable. Was this exercise in private investigation worth the effort? I would say yes; yes, it was. This effort was actually fun. Having a hunch and following it through to successful completion was satisfying, especially since it involved the greatest guitarist of all time, Jimi Hendrix.

9

GUITAR MAN, MYTH, LEGEND

In 1997 I parted with my guitar collection to finance the purchase of my first home. This included a 1958 Les Paul Standard Sunburst in near mint condition that I bought in 1980 for $8,000. This was one of the finest-sounding and most beautiful instruments, and the maple wood top had rare birds-eye figuring in it. I drove all the way to Santa Barbara to buy that guitar in 1980. Everyone said I was out of my mind and that I would never see my money back because I had paid more than those guitars were selling for at the time. They were wrong. Seventeen years later I sold it for $50,000. Today it would probably be worth $250,000. At the time I was thinking, "I should buy ten or twenty of these." A couple of people I know did just that—and, if they still have them, they did quite well.

From 1968 through 1998 the prices of vintage guitars just kept rising for the simple reason that a growing pool of collectors, investors, and rock stars were buying them. And when I purchased my house in 1998, the dot-com bubble economy was booming and I continued to accumulate a good deal of money. To a veteran guitar dealer and collector, it represented a real opportunity.

"I can really leverage the money that I've earned," I told myself. "Imagine how many guitars I can buy!" For the first time I could purchase a good number of valuable instruments all at once. Simply put, I could accumulate a new collection in a fraction of the time it had taken to build my first.

With that goal I began looking for entire guitar collections for sale and found a lot of promising possibilities. After all, I was one of only a few dealers with the capital to purchase a complete collection, lock, stock, and barrel. It was, and still is, a very unusual business strategy. Most dealers are not interested in buying every guitar in someone's guitar collection. They would rather cherry-pick the best instruments and leave the rest for someone else who might not be as discerning. My approach was different: I would buy the whole collection and sell the most valuable to recoup my initial investment. The rest—the so-called "less desirable" instruments—would still have considerable value and together could be sold for a handsome profit.

So began my adventures in buying entire guitar collections. My first was a sterling 135-piece collection owned by a dealer in Reno, Nevada. From there I picked up many smaller lots: twenty pieces, fifty pieces, seventy-five pieces . . . whatever came my way that made financial sense. But buying the fabled Chinery guitar collection was far and away my most notable accomplishment.

Scott Chinery founded a health food company in the eighties that he ended up selling for north of $100 million ten years later. A passionate guitar aficionado, Mr. Chinery spent three dizzying years on a worldwide guitar-buying spree, purchasing every great guitar he could find, with a special emphasis on classic arch-top jazz instruments. I had run across the ads he placed in prominent guitar magazines under the headline "The Search Is On!" And, while guitars were not the only thing he collected (he even owned one of the original Batmobiles, the original Batcycle, and several vintage Ferraris), guitars represented by far his most noteworthy avocation.

Scott Chinery could afford to indulge his passion. Flamboyant and smart, he lived in a mansion, moved in the left lane, and knew how to enjoy his wealth. No question, Scott was charismatic and fun to be around, with a reputation as a consummate prankster. When it came to collecting vintage guitars, he was knowledgeable, yet ultimately did not have quite the experience and expertise to make the best decisions on his own. Once he launched his global vintage guitar search, he hired someone to help build his collection—and that person turned out to be somewhat less than honest. The outcome was predictable.

More than a few of Scott's guitars were not the finest examples of a given model. Some of them had condition problems and provenance issues. And he had paid inflated prices to acquire a number of these instruments. Rumor was that the dealer he'd retained would buy a valuable instrument with Scott's money and then keep it, purchasing a lesser example to foist off on Scott. As a result, the millionaire collector did not have as many premium pieces as his riches could have afforded, despite the fact that he often paid top dollar.

That said, Scott still managed to amass an amazing collection of over seven hundred guitars in those three whirlwind years. His love of guitars prompted him to help promote the instrument as an item of twentieth-century iconography. His collection was immortalized in a lavish book titled *The Chinery Collection: 150 Years of American Guitars*. The Smithsonian Institution mounted an exhibition on guitars that highlighted a significant portion of his collection. Scott hoped to do for guitars what had been done with other forms of fine craftsmanship and artwork: to create an appreciation among the general population. All told, Mr. Chinery's contribution to the world of guitars was extraordinary.

Sadly and unexpectedly, Scott Chinery died in October 2000 of a heart attack at the young age of forty. I must admit that his death put my own lifelong obsession with guitars and guitar collecting into a new perspective. Scott had been on top of the world: happily married, father of four children, with all the wealth he could ever need, and proud possessor of one of the finest guitar collections ever assembled. Then, suddenly, it was all over. Scott's passing served as a somber measure of priorities in life.

Nevertheless, I had been actively searching for a formidable collection to purchase, and it was common knowledge that Scott Chinery had put together the ultimate assemblage of rare and precious instruments. While he was still alive, there was little merit in approaching him with an offer on his collection. But after his death, I wondered whether his family would have the same emotional investment in the guitars. I told myself that, after the appropriate passage of time, I would contact Scott's widow to see what she intended to do with his collection.

After waiting over a year for the right time, I heard rumors that Mrs. Chinery had entered into discussions with some major auction houses—Christie's and Sotheby's, to be exact—to sell her late husband's guitars. I also picked up a valuable piece of inside information: Scott had been planning to sell his collection before he died. "Zounds," I said. It was time to make my move.

Trying urgently to get in touch with Mrs. Chinery, I kept running into one dead end after another. I could not establish direct contact, nor could I find anyone who actually knew her. It seemed Mrs. Chinery was a virtual recluse, not listed in the phone book, not available via e-mail, with no known address—at least none that I could run down.

Finally, a friend of mine, the noted guitar dealer Larry Wexer, got word to me that his friend Larry Acunto, editor of *Twentieth Century Guitar* and one of Scott's closest compatriots in the realm of collecting fine instruments, was acquainted with Mrs. Chinery. "What's in it for us," they both wanted to know, "if we make this deal happen?"

I made them an offer, and, properly motivated, they made the necessary phone calls.

"She's interested," I was told a few days later, "but she's already in serious discussions with Christie's and Sotheby's about putting together an auction." Had I gotten into the game too late?

Christie's and Sotheby's are the world's largest auction houses. I would have to work quickly and effectively to thwart their goal of auctioning Scott's collection, especially since either of these highly reputable firms could certainly and quickly close a deal with Mrs. Chinery.

"Get us in the door," I implored my contacts, "and please get us a meeting as quickly as you can." The back-and-forth went on for weeks, until finally I got a call from Larry Acunto.

"I've talked to Mrs. Chinery," he told me, "and she's ready to meet with you this Tuesday morning at nine o'clock at her attorney's office in New Jersey."

The phone call came on a Sunday night, and by Tuesday morning I was on the East Coast for what proved to be one of the most important business meetings of my life.

Ahead of our meeting, Mrs. Chinery had sent a list of all the guitars in the Chinery collection. As I perused it, in the back of my mind was the sum for which I knew, through another party, Scott had already privately offered to sell his collection. I mentally tallied the approximate cost of his massive inventory, more than seven hundred guitars, stored in climate-controlled conditions in Mrs. Chinery's expansive New Jersey mansion.

The recently completed estate had a 7,500-square-foot, fully hu-
midified basement still under construction at the time of Scott's
death, but now packed with vintage guitars of every stripe.
When I arrived at the office of Mrs. Chinery's lawyer, he introduced himself and laid out ground rules before the owner even
entered the room.

"You should know that we are not ready to make a deal on
this collection as yet," he told me, "but if our meeting goes well,
we are willing to proceed step by step in good faith. If at the end
of the day you have the best offer on the table, we will conclude
the deal with you. If not, we won't. It's as simple as that."

I was ushered into a conference room to finally meet Mrs.
Chinery face to face. I had thought about this deal for a long
time and had a picture in my mind of what Kathy Chinery would
look like. It seems I am always wrong when I try to envision
what people look like before meeting them in person. But this
time I was right! Kathy was thin, blonde, and quite attractive. I
attempted to address Mrs. Chinery before the meeting began
in earnest, but I was quickly, though kindly, interrupted by her
lawyer. I knew my strength had always been my ability to close
a deal, but I also could see that Mrs. Chinery's advisors and
legal counsel were going to ensure this would be anything but
easy. The patented Guitar Man technique that had worked so
well on so many occasions was not going to play a big part in
these negotiations. Had I wasted my time traveling all the way
to New Jersey? Was I on a fool's errand?

It felt that way as the meeting started on a tense note. Six
of us sat around a huge conference table. It was immediately
apparent that Mrs. Chinery was still bereft over the loss of her
husband. She knew the collection had been his passion, and
it seemed that she was distraught at the thought that selling
would sever an important tie. Under those circumstances,

My friend Jun Iwata holding the 1955 Strat I purchased from Quentin Daly. When I discovered it was worth far more than what I paid for it, I sent Quentin a check for the difference, but he refused to cash it, saying, "A deal's a deal, son." (Photos by Michael Indelicato)

The 1958 Gibson Les Paul Standard I acquired from Willard "Fleetwood" Brougham in 2004. Sealing the deal for this stunner involved months of chauffeuring, the purchase of an unwanted scooter, and a proposed marriage to Brougham's lovely stepdaughter. (Author's collection)

1968 Rosewood Fender Stratocaster. One of the most beautiful Fender guitars ever produced—and one of the most historic. I am fully convinced that it was the guitar made by Fender to present as a gift to Jimi Hendrix. (Photos courtesy of the Chicago Music Exchange)

Scott Chinery with his fabulous collection, circa 1996. Scott put together an amazing collection of over seven hundred guitars. (Author's collection)

The Larson Brothers "Big Boy" acoustic guitar, 1935—one of the many jewels of the Chinery collection. (Photo by Michael Indelicato)

1992 D'Aquisto Advance. Considered a masterpiece by one of the great luthiers, James D'Aquisto. One of the great guitars I acquired as a part of the Scott Chinery collection. (Photo by Michael Indelicato)

1992 D'Aquisto Teardrop. Another amazing instrument by Mr. D'Aquisto. This guitar was custom built for Mr. Chinery and part of his exquisite collection. (Photo by Michael Indelicato)

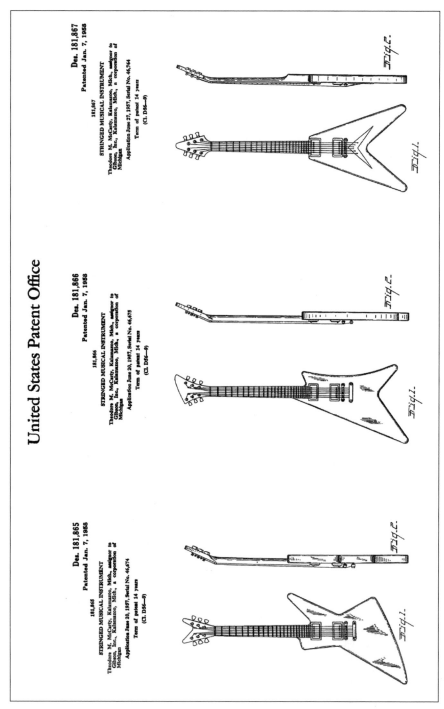

Original patent drawings for the Gibson Explorer, Flying V, and Moderne, circa 1957. These are copies of the original drawings that were submitted to the United States Patent Office.

the sale of the Chinery collection was about more than just money.

It was a situation I had been in many times, and I could recall many others who had had great difficulty selling instruments. For some, their guitar was a most prized possession, an irreplaceable family heirloom. For others, the guitar represented memories of carefree youth and the great music that had been an important passion of their lives. For still others, selling a guitar that had belonged to a deceased husband or son felt like a betrayal, a connection forever broken as soon as the instrument walked out the door.

As this meeting began and I listened to Mrs. Chinery reminisce about her deceased husband, I tried my best to comprehend her cares and concerns. I also had firsthand knowledge of what her husband had felt about his guitars—the pride, passion, and love he had invested in all of them. It was a matter of the heart with which I was only too familiar.

As we talked I started to better understand Mrs. Chinery's objectives. She had asked me to call her by her first name, and I took that as a hopeful sign. Mostly I attempted to find out what would make her comfortable with a proposed deal and what would alleviate any primary issues. So I listened carefully to what she had to say. Then I asked a few questions.

"Assuming you move forward with selling the collection," I began, "how would you propose to proceed?"

"I would like it to be quick," she replied quietly. "I want to minimize the impact on my family and me—and on the memories of my husband." She went on to tell me she did not want to sell the guitars one by one, since it would in all likelihood take years to finish that task. I agreed with her on that point.

"I would also like it to be accomplished without a lot of publicity," she added. "But, most importantly, I don't want any unnecessary complications: the simpler the better. We set a price. We agree to that price. Then it's done."

I realized, my own agenda aside, I would truly be the best buyer for her, better by far than an auction sale.

"If you are contemplating an auction," I told her, "then you are in for a very long and protracted negotiating process with these auction houses that will be vying to represent your collection and your interests, as well as their own. And it will be anything but low-profile. It's to the benefit of any auction house to generate as much awareness of the sale as possible. The very nature of a public auction entails a tremendous amount of publicity and advertising. Everyone in the guitar-collecting world is going to know who you are and what you're doing. You will be in constant contact with the auction house agents until the collection is sold.

"You should also know that your husband accumulated a lot of guitars in his collection that I assume are going to need maintenance and repair work prior to being sold. And, perhaps most importantly, many of these instruments may not sell at auction, at least for the reserve you might set.

"If you're interested in a one-stop buyer," I summed up, "a person who walks in, inspects the guitars, hands you a cashier's check, then loads up the guitars and takes them home, then I'm your man."

Mrs. Chinery glanced at her lawyer and then turned back to me. "That's exactly what I want," she said. "But at what price?"

This was the crucial moment. Since I already knew the price that Scott had been willing to consider for his collection while he was still alive, I used this as the baseline for my offer. Mrs. Chinery looked impressed, as if realizing I had done my homework. After conferring with her attorney in a whisper, she asked if I could give them a few minutes to talk alone.

That few minutes ended up being a nerve-racking three-quarters of an hour. As I waited, Larry Acunto sidled up to me and admitted he had never seen anything quite like the way I had cut to the chase. "That was smooth!" he said admiringly. "I'll bet she's going to do it. You're going to own this collection."

"Thanks," I replied, "I hope you're right." But when Mrs. Chinery and her representatives filed back into the conference room, I could see by the look on their faces that it was not yet a done deal.

"Michael," she said after we took our seats again, "if we agree to your offer, I just want to make sure I'm getting a fair price for this collection. I know, and you know, that this is approximately the price that Scott himself wanted. But that was several years ago. We want to be sure about what the fair market value of the collection is today."

"OK," I responded earnestly, "if we can agree to this price, I will give you an unconditional right of rescission. In the interim, if you want to get the collection appraised, you'll have that opportunity. A good appraisal would work to both our benefits. But please tell whatever appraiser you retain that you want the honest market value and ask what the retail and wholesale value of the collection will be. That's very important.

"I'm being totally candid with you," I continued. "I'm not going to buy Scott's collection to keep for myself. If I had the money I might do exactly that, but I don't have extra millions of dollars lying around to invest, no matter how much I'd like to keep these guitars together. What I'm going to do is sell enough of them to recoup my investment and keep the ones I can afford to hang onto. The price I've offered you will allow me to do just that. I think it is going to be a very good deal for both of us."

The bottom line was as simple as I could make it: I was asking her to trust that I was offering her a fair price and underlining my good faith by allowing her to conduct an appraisal. It was a formula that seemed to satisfy both our interests.

"All right," she said, and I could tell she was warming to the idea. "One of the few dealers that Scott really trusted in the vintage guitar business is sitting in this room right now." She turned to Larry Wexer. "Larry," she said, "if you give me an objective appraisal of this collection and it is in the ballpark of Michael's offer, then I'll be satisfied."

"Absolutely," Larry said, "I'll be happy to." Admittedly, there was a conflict of interest in the arrangement, since Larry would be getting a commission from me if this deal were completed. I told Mrs. Chinery this, but she dismissed it. "I trust Larry."

The meeting concluded with a handshake. We had cut the deal for the collection, even though they had said that it wouldn't happen at the outset of the meeting. It just goes to show how closing any deal is a sensitive matter. It takes a two-pronged approach. First, you have to listen to people and intuit what *they* most want to happen. That is critical in getting anyone to agree to a proposal. What works for them is as important as what works for you. Then, you have to encourage them to make the next move, applying a little pressure if they are sitting on the fence, leery of making what could be a very important financial and emotional decision. In the case of Mrs. Chinery, any decision would carry both personal and financial implications. So I listened to her and her lawyer and attempted to provide what they wanted. In the end, they reciprocated.

They wanted a $1,000,000 deposit before we could walk through to preview and hopefully approve the guitars. If we weren't satisfied, they would refund the money. If we were satisfied, we were to deposit the balance in an account and the guitars were ours. I brought a team of half a dozen specialized guitar experts with me to New Jersey and spent two days going through the instruments. I was tested on every front of my guitar knowledge because there were so many different makes and models. Some were beautiful and some had problems. Overall, it was a remarkable collection and a great deal.

A week later, my team and I packed and loaded more than seven hundred guitars and amplifiers from the basement of the Chinery mansion. It took six people almost five hours to remove all the instruments and equipment from the Chinery estate and pack it into the moving van parked out front. This daunting task demanded the utmost care. Afterwards, I flew to California to prepare to receive the collection. Because I did not have nearly enough space to house it all, I had to get back and immediately find a place to accommodate this massive new purchase. Fortunately, I located an appropriate facility, a warehouse space in San Rafael, a picturesque town in Marin County. Meanwhile, a fifty-two-foot, humidity-controlled semi was on the move across the country day and night, with driver and crew stopping only for food and fuel. Once they got the collection to California, we had to be ready to unload all the guitars quickly, a considerable chore. In the end, my storage facility was so packed with guitars that there was hardly room to turn around in its now cramped confines.

To inspect and catalog seven hundred guitars was a Herculean amount of work, far more than the collections of a hundred or so guitars I had bought before. This was much more difficult in terms of logistics; cleaning, repairing, and even the menial task of changing strings on seven hundred guitars was a huge undertaking—more than I had ever anticipated. Some of the guitars hadn't been touched in ten years, so there were corrosion issues and some potentiometers had seized on the electric guitars. Each one of them needed to be cleaned, polished, and attended to.

But that was only the beginning of my challenges with the Chinery collection. Once I started selling off individual guitars, I found there were more than a few problem instruments among the authentic treasures. The collection's 1958 Gibson Flying V, for instance, ended up being a total fake—for which I had paid $70,000. I contacted the dealer who had sold it to Scott, and, predictably, he refused to take responsibility. There was nothing I could do but accept that a forgery had been passed along to me. I sucked it up and took the hit.

At the end of the day, while the deal was still very profitable, there were other problematic aspects to the historic purchase. Over the course of my career, I have never really had any major difficulties with other dealers, but when I bought the Chinery collection, a few of my colleagues were resentful. Call it professional jealousy. Most of them either wanted first crack at the best guitars or wanted to be part of the deal. Their aggrieved attitude was unexpected and, at the time, truly awkward. I attribute the situation to my own failure to be proactive with fellow dealers: to let them know what I was doing up front.

Since I bought the Chinery guitars, another major player has put together an even more impressive collection, but Scott's collection will always remain unique. Through his collection, and in the pages of his book, Scott tried to tell the story of the American guitar, starting with an 1833 Martin presentation guitar, all the way through the best examples of twentieth-century guitar craftsmanship. He had arch-tops specifically built for him by Jimmy D'Aquisto, a master builder, as well as by other leading luthiers. In fact, Scott had the world's best collection of guitars made by both D'Aquisto and another legendary guitar maker, John D'Angelico; they were the brilliant highlights of his collection. I can still remember opening the case to the D'Aquisto Teardrop, with a body that was shaped like a graceful tear, as well as laying eyes on a one-of-a-kind D'Aquisto Advance for the first time, and simply being astounded. In that regard, Scott's collection was unmatched in telling an important story of great American artistry.

Scott's collection of fifty Gibson Super 400s, the company's top-of-the-line jazz guitar, was singular. Similarly, he had a great collection of Martin and Larson Brothers Flattop guitars. And his four 1960 Les Paul Standards were superb examples of that classic model. The 1958 Rick Derringer–owned Gibson V-Headstock Explorer was probably the most valuable guitar in the collection, but Scott had some amazing Fender instruments as well, such as a 1955 shell-pink Precision Bass with a matching pink thumb rest. There were also some amazing Stratocasters, twenty-seven custom-colored Jazz Masters, and . . . well, let's just say that the list goes on.

Perhaps, from an investment perspective, Scott would have been better served to focus on postwar Fender electric guitars, Gibson solid-body electrics, and 1930–1940 Martin guitars. But the collection was still a fabulous accomplishment. And so, for that matter, was being able to buy it all in one piece. To date, it is the largest guitar transaction in history—both in number of instruments sold and dollar amount paid. It presented both unique opportunities and unique challenges. A guitar collector recently asked me whether, if I had to do it over again, I would still buy the Chinery collection, or would recommend such a purchase to other dealers. I replied that the answer to the first question was *yes* and the answer to the second was *no*.

10

HOLY GRAIL, WHERE ART THOU?

In the world of vintage guitars, there are many objects of fervent desire. But nothing better qualifies as the collector's holy grail than the elusive Gibson "Moderne." This almost mythical instrument was supposedly built in 1957 as a prototype for the modernistic guitar line slated for introduction to the market by Gibson in 1958. Made from African limba wood—called "Korina" by the company—the product line included the Moderne, the Flying V, and the Explorer. Gibson manufactured approximately 100 flying V's and 40 Explorers. Yet only two Modernes were ever made— or so the story goes.

Gibson was keen to release this so-called modernistic guitar line. Each of the new models was premised on the concept of cutting-edge, futuristic design. In 1957, the notion of space travel and sleek aeronautical design was certainly in vogue. The Sputnik space capsule was circling the globe in October of that same year, and there can be no question that the Explorer (shaped like a lightning bolt), the Moderne (shaped like Gumby), and the Flying V (shaped like the "flying wing" aircraft) were designed with these new sensibilities in mind.

With the release of the futuristic Stratocaster in 1954, the upstart Fender Corporation had trumped Gibson and challenged its supremacy. Not wanting to be left behind, Gibson hastened to produce a new line that not only looked more radical than Leo Fender's successful Stratocaster but also, being constructed of light-colored limba wood, would show up prominently on the black-and-white television screens that were the standard at that time. So when Gibson brought the Explorer and the Flying V to the market, they were taken aback by the paltry orders they received from their dealers. After it became clear these instruments were a flop, Gibson quickly folded the Explorer and the Flying V. The guitars were ahead of their time.

Regarding the Moderne, some say it existed only as a concept drawing. Others claim the guitar was manufactured and sold, but in such limited numbers as to be virtually extinct today.

Like so many others, I have been fascinated by the mystery of the Moderne. I even traveled to Hawaii to meet the former president of Gibson, Mr. Ted McCarty, who headed up the company from 1948 to 1966 and was the moving creative force in Gibson's revitalization. In decline when McCarty took the helm, the company became the undisputed market leader during his tenure. The innovations and new designs developed during the McCarty era included the pioneering humbucking pickup, the Les Paul guitar, the ES-335 line, the S.G. guitars, the Firebird series, and the signature series guitars such as the Trini Lopez model. Mr. McCarty also designed the line of modernistic guitars.

His is an impressive list of groundbreaking instruments. For those not familiar with these guitars or the terminology, it is enough to know that Ted McCarty made Gibson a household name and oversaw the manufacture of the finest guitars the company ever produced. Today, the "McCarty era" is synonymous with Gibson's "golden age."

Except for his legacy of innovation at Gibson, I knew very little about Mr. McCarty. I had only seen a picture of him at his desk at the Gibson corporate headquarters back in the fifties; he appeared to be a large and imposing man with a confident demeanor. A friend told me that he had retired to Hawaii and that I might be able to find his phone number in the Maui telephone book. Sure enough, he was listed. I wasted no time in calling and telling Ted what a big fan I was of his work and legacy. Would it be possible to come to Maui to discuss the Gibson line of modernistic guitars?

"Of course," he replied. "It would be a pleasure to have you over."

Arriving at Ted's well-appointed condominium on the lush paradise island of Maui, I was amazed to be greeted by a gentleman no more than a few inches over five feet tall. But it didn't take long to realize that, while he may have been slight of stature, he had a giant personality and similarly outsized executive abilities. He was an impressive man and all the more remarkable considering that Ted was then eighty-six years old. Yet Mr. McCarty retained a razor-sharp memory, and, after several hours of free-ranging conversation sitting around the swimming pool, I worked up the gumption to ask the question I had come all that way to put to him.

"Was the Moderne guitar ever actually built?"

His answer came without hesitation. "Yes," he assured me. "We built two and we took one to the N.A.M.M. trade show in New York in 1957. The guitar got a bad response from our retail vendors, but we had a positive reaction with the Explorer and even more so with the Flying V, so we put those two into production and scrapped the Moderne."

"So, to the best of your recollection," I persisted, "the Moderne was actually built?"

"Absolutely, it was built," he shot back, a little put out that I would question his memory. "I know it. I saw it."

Ted went on to suggest that the two prototype guitars probably had been given to a sales representative after the N.A.M.M. show and either sold to a store somewhere, or perhaps kept as a souvenir by the salesman. He certainly led me to believe that somewhere out there in the wide world—in a closet, in an attic, or under someone's bed—lurks a guitar that is perhaps the most supremely rare, historic, and valuable fretted instrument in existence.

What makes the Moderne the holy grail of guitars? The answer is simple: it has never been found! I am sure, if one ever did surface, the mystique would be diminished. But until then, it remains every collector's fantasy. Gibson did reissue a copy of the Moderne in the early 1980s, but those original 1957 Moderne prototypes have since been fodder for endless gossip, especially since no one knows exactly what became of them.

The 1958 Gibson Explorer is the guitar most commonly considered to be next on the holy grail list, right below the mythical Moderne. Certainly it is the most coveted and rarest of all the Gibson electric guitars. Of the original forty or so manufactured in 1958, fewer than twenty good examples in original condition are known to exist. Over the years, I've had only a few opportunities to purchase a 1958 Explorer.

In 1985 I got a letter from Guitar Trader, a well-respected vintage guitar dealer in New Jersey, telling me they had just received a 1958 Gibson Explorer with a V-shaped head stock. There was only one known original example of this guitar, and I knew that it had belonged to the virtuoso guitarist/songwriter Rick Derringer, who had owned and played it in the 1970s. Rick believes he first saw the guitar at the Gibson factory when his dad took him on a tour there in 1958.

"I always had this fantasy that it was the same guitar I saw in that glass case," said Mr. Derringer, who purchased this legendary instrument in 1971, some thirteen years after he first saw it at the Gibson factory in Kalamazoo, Michigan. I believe that he was correct; it had to be the same guitar, because there is only one known "V" headstock Explorer ever confirmed to be original. Sadly, a number of fakes have traded hands, leading to litigation and dashed hopes.

I truly wanted to purchase the V headstock Explorer from Guitar Trader in 1985, but couldn't afford the $8,000 price tag at that time because I was still in college. Eighteen years later, in 2003, it came around to me again as part of the Chinery collection. I thus became the proud owner of this historic instrument.

A few years earlier, another Gibson Explorer had crossed my path. I received a call in 1996 from Mark Kremer, a guitar dealer from Northern California with whom I had done business.

"I know where there is an original 1958 Explorer," Mark told me. "It's here in Sacramento. I've just seen it. It has never been altered and even has the original case. It's in very good condition. The owner is going to sell it to me for $20,000 and I'm going to ask $75,000 for it."

"I don't care what you pay for it," I replied. "I only care what I have to pay for it." It was then that Mark let drop that he didn't have the $20,000 to finance the purchase price.

"Well, I do," I replied. "I'll front you the 20K so you can buy the guitar. Then, after you get it, I'll pay you the balance." We shook hands, and it was a done deal.

A few days later, I gave Mark the $20,000 in cash. He called the next day to tell me he'd purchased the Explorer, and it was safely locked in his closet. Now I had to get busy and raise the other $55,000 to complete the payment for the guitar. I surmised that it would take me about three weeks to raise the capital. Mark also insisted that he wanted to be paid in cash, so I went to the additional effort to get the 55K together in greenbacks.

Meanwhile, Mark kept calling to say, "You better have that money for me on time."

"Relax, palooka," I said, "The cash is coming."

And, just as planned, a couple of weeks later, after selling a few prized guitars, I had patched together the funds to pay the balance on the Explorer. I was ready to go up and take possession of this icon.

Finally, the day I was to deliver the money, I called Mark to give him the heads-up that I was en route with a bulging briefcase full of Benjamins.

Mark Kremer was a nice enough fellow. Obviously, I trusted him enough to advance him $20,000 on the purchase of the '58 Explorer before he even had the guitar in hand. But when you put so much effort, trust, and cash into an arrangement like this, you begin to question your own judgment. Then you begin to question the motives of the people you are doing business with.

Mark fancied himself a biker. While not an outlaw, he did run with some fellows who were known to ride choppers and perhaps dabble in socially unacceptable behavior. And even though I trusted Mark, I would be telling an untruth if I were to suggest that I wasn't a bit nervous as I packed that money into my briefcase for the one-and-a-half-hour trip to Sacramento.

What if the guitar was a fake? What if it had been refinished? I would then be in the unenviable position of having made a huge effort to raise all this money for naught. And if I rejected the guitar, the situation would be even more complicated. Since Mark didn't have much money in those days, how would I recover the $20,000 that I had forwarded to him as a deposit on the guitar? These thoughts were in my mind as I got on Interstate 80, headed in the direction of the California state capital.

When I arrived at Mark's residence, there it was, right in front of me, an honest-to-goodness holy grail: a 1958 Gibson Explorer in its original case. The guitar wasn't quite as pristine as I had been led to believe. Don't get me wrong, it was still a great instrument, but in all honesty, I was mildly disappointed by the amount of playing wear on its surface. All things considered, it *was* an original 1958 Explorer, a guitar just about impossible to find, so the deal was consummated.

I started counting out the $55,000 to add to the $20,000 I had given Mark earlier. For me, this represented a major investment in a single instrument. It took us an hour to count and recount the money, as I forked over stacks of hundreds in piles totaling $1,000 each. With the task finally completed, I thanked Mark and carefully carried the Explorer out to my van. It was an introspective ninety-minute drive back to the Bay Area as I turned the transaction over in my mind. I kept asking myself, "Am I crazy to spend $75,000 for a guitar?"

The next morning I awoke to find a message from Mark Kremer waiting on my answering machine with a time stamp of four in the morning. In a distressed tone, Mark asked me to call him. What was this about? With an uneasy feeling in the pit of my stomach, I punched in his number.

"What did you do after you left my house?" he asked immediately in a decidedly inquisitorial tone.

"I went home and I went to bed," I told him. "It was after midnight by the time I got here. What else would I do?"

"Why didn't you answer your phone?" he demanded.

"Why? Because it was four a.m. and I was counting sheep," I said, with more than a hint of sarcasm. "What's going on, Mark?"

It was then that he related his harrowing tale. "Someone broke into my place after you left," he explained breathlessly. "They held me at gunpoint and tried to rob me. I'm sure they knew about all the cash you brought for the Explorer."

At first I thought he was joking, but he continued: "The guy beat the shit out of me. He pistol-whipped me and I thought he was going to kill me. He didn't find the money, but he knew I had it, that's for sure. He kept beating on me and asking, 'Where is it? Where is it?' Then he would hit me some more." There was a long pause on the line.

"Sure, Mark," I said sardonically. "Sure."

"I'm dead serious," he replied. "Did you have anything to do with this?"

I was dumbstruck by his accusation. "You gotta be joking," I said, but I could tell from the lack of response that there was nothing funny about the situation from Mark's perspective. But it seemed too weird and unlikely to be true. How could anybody else have known he was sitting on that huge stash of cash?

After doing my best to calm him down, I quickly called a mutual friend to find out more about Mark's allegation. Was it even true that he'd been assaulted?

"He sure was," the friend confirmed. "The guy made hamburger out of him, but Mark wasn't about to give him the money. Fortunately, he had already hidden it really well."

Over the next few days Mark continued to view me as the instigator of this attempted home invasion robbery. He called several of my friends and business associates asking if I was capable of hatching such a plot.

Finally, I got a clue as to what had actually happened when another guitar collector in the area gave me a call. "I just heard a little story that I thought you might like to know," he said. "Mark Kremer was going around town just before he sold you that Explorer, telling everyone that he was buying it for $20,000 and selling it for $75,000."

"That's right," I replied. "That was our deal."

"That may have been your deal," the collector continued, "but what Mark told the guy he bought it from was that he could only sell it for $25,000. That was a big mistake, because this dude happens to be a biker and a member of a very well-recognized motorcycle gang."

Armed with this new information, I promptly called Mark, intending to let him know that I had a pretty good idea of who had visited him that evening and why. "Did you tell anyone what our actual deal was?" I demanded.

After trying to play it down, he finally came clean.

"Well," I replied, "did it ever occur to you that the owner of the guitar was trying to get his hands on all the profit you made after you lied to him about how much you could sell the guitar for?"

"It's possible," he acknowledged reluctantly.

"So do you still think I hired some goombah to bust you up and steal the money?"

There was only silence from Mark's end except for the obnoxious sound of a parrot in the background.

It took a long time for Mr. Kremer to at last confess his mistake, finally calling about six months later to apologize. "Sorry, man," he said. "I was wrong. I talked to some dude who knew the guys who tried to rob me, and it was the guy who I bought the guitar from. Mike, I wrongly suspected you and I'm sorry."

Mark was fortunate to escape the whole escapade with a few bruises and a bad headache. I suspect the disgruntled biker or one of his confederates had been outside his house that night, watching me walk in with a briefcase full of cash and walk out with the guitar. I was very lucky that I wasn't rolled then and there for the fifty-five grand, the Explorer, or both.

But the story did not end there. A few weeks later, I started getting suspicious calls at my house.

"I hear you buy guitars, man," said the voice over the line.

"Who did you hear that from?" I asked.

"Somebody gave me your number," was the reply. "I got an old Fender guitar for sale that you might want to buy." The phone call was originating in the 916 area code—Sacramento.

With real misgivings, but never willing to pass up a possible deal, I told him to come over. The guy who showed up later that day looked like he had just gotten out of Folsom prison, covered in tattoos. He had a cheap guitar in his hand, but he seemed less interested in selling it than he did in checking out my inventory. He was accompanied by a girl who had the hollow eyes, stinky breath, and bad teeth of a meth addict.

"Show me some of your guitars, homey," he suggested. "What you got? What's your most expensive one?"

Fortunately, at the time I didn't have any instruments around, since I was in the midst of remodeling and the entire house was empty.

"I don't have them here," I replied. "I keep my guitars in storage. I never have them just lying around the house."

The guy grunted and traded a look with his girlfriend, and they took off. To this day, I am convinced that they came down to case my house for a possible robbery. And, even though I cannot prove it, I am equally convinced that they were somehow tied in with the nice folks who attacked Mark.

The entire episode was one of the strangest, most unnerving and potentially dangerous that I have ever experienced in my long career as a dealer and collector. Roughly a year later, I sold the '58 Explorer that I had purchased from Mark Kremer. It went for $80,000—a meager $5,000 profit.

Incidentally, in 1999 I was able to buy another 1958 Gibson

Explorer from a fellow in Santa Barbara. He told me it was the "Bangladesh Explorer," but I didn't really know what that meant. When my friend Mike Parker, of the Van Horn adventure, discovered I had this instrument, he was so excited he couldn't sleep until I agreed to sell it to him. Only after I sold him the guitar did I learn the full history of that '58 Explorer and the Concert for Bangladesh.

After a 1970 tidal wave killed hundreds of thousands in the country of Bangladesh, next door to India, George Harrison and other musicians put together a concert and live-album recording to raise relief money. It was a huge success and a forerunner of efforts such as Live Aid. This 1958 Explorer guitar, owned by Leon Russell's guitar player Don Preston at the time, was played by George Harrison, Eric Clapton, and other stars at the Bangladesh Concert. With a pedigree like that, if I had done my research in time, I might have held on to this guitar or sold it for a lot more money later. It was one of the most important instruments I ever owned.

Had I retained ownership of these two Explorers for ten more years, they would have become *really* good investments. By 2007, I learned of several transactions of original '58 Explorers selling for over $400,000. At the end of the day, the Explorer that I purchased from Mark Kremer left me with several valuable lessons: (1) Be careful from whom you buy your holy grail; (2) Loose lips sink ships; and (3) Don't ever sell a grail!

11

SEPARATION ANXIETY

Cash is king in many transactions, especially when other buyers or dealers turn a sale into a bidding war. I remember a perfect example of this phenomenon that began with a call from a gentleman in Redding, California, regarding a 1957 Gibson Super 400 CESN. The man said the guitar was in excellent condition and he wanted $7,000, which was a really sweet deal at that time. "Gotta be all cash!" he said before he gave me the directions to his home. As I was about to leave for the drive up to Redding, I noticed in the Modesto paper that someone else was selling a Fender Telecaster guitar for $2,000. I thought that was a high price for a Telecaster, unless, of course, it was an older vintage model. So I called the owner and left a message.

The three-hour trek to Redding was rewarding. The 1957 Gibson Super 400 was amazing, absolutely unplayed, with original strings, even original wrapping paper, and it still smelled new. It was simply perfect, the best one in existence. I wanted to keep this guitar for my collection (though I often felt that way about any great guitar I picked up).

The owner of that guitar had received it as an eighteenth birthday present in early 1958—and he still had the photos of him holding the guitar on that fateful day. The guitar case for this beauty even had a case cover that was also in perfect condition. With "Alnico" pickups—named for their powerful magnets and their "see-through" natural finish—this was one of the rarest and most beautiful vintage Gibson guitars ever produced. Inside its case it even had the little Gibson screwdriver provided from the factory to adjust the intonation of the bridge. The whole package was like a time capsule, a stunning find.

As I was driving back from Redding, the Modesto Telecaster owner called back and said hers was a 1953 Telecaster that her father had owned. I told her that if it was truly that year and model, I would take it at $2,000, and would be there in three hours. $2,000 was a great price—almost too good to be true. What a day!

However, since I had just bought the Super 400 Gibson for $7,000 I had only about $1,500 left in my pocket that afternoon. And since it was a Sunday and the banks were closed, my fear was that someone else would see the ad in the Modesto paper, call, and snatch it out from under me. How was I going to get that extra $500? It was hammer down as I raced at eighty miles an hour all the way down the interstate, hoping that I could figure out a way to acquire the '53 Tele.

When I arrived, the owner invited me in to see the guitar. She seemed a little nervous, and, when after a quick inspection I said, "Cool, this is great; I'll take it," she prevaricated: "Well, somebody else called and they want to come over and look at it first. And I told them that before I sold it I would let them have a look at it."

I knew exactly what that meant; it meant that the other prospective buyer had suggested that he would pay above and beyond the asking price listed in the newspaper. So it was time to play hardball. "No," I said. "No. I just drove three hours to get here and you told me in the clearest terms that I could have it for $2,000. That, sister, is known as a binding legal contract."

Trouble was, I was short $500, so I said, "Listen, I've got $1,500, which I'll leave you; then I'll come back in the morning with the rest of the cash."

"No. I think I'll just wait."

She refused. It was her turn to play a little hardball with me. So I tried another avenue: "O.K., I'll give you this $1,500 now and call some friends who will come with the rest of the money. I'm buying this guitar right here and now—just like I said I would. A deal is a deal."

The fact of the matter is that this lady was not a crook, just someone who had not done her research on her father's instrument and had listed it for sale at a price lower than what it was worth. This is a common mistake, and it has happened to all of us—including me—numerous times. At that point she had little choice but to agree. She hesitantly said, "Okay, get me the money." But right then there was a knock at the door: Steve, another vintage guitar collector, walked in with a look of nervous anticipation. He strolled right past me with a phony, tight-lipped smile, opened the case of the guitar, gave it the once-over, and said, "I want it. I got the money right here." He pulled out a wad of hundred-dollar bills as a shot over the bow.

The owner of the guitar knew that she had me over a barrel.

"Well, I guess he's got the money. First one with the money gets it—unless you want to raise your offer."

This was a hell of a predicament.

"No," I said to Steve. "Oh, no, this is not right. I've been around the track a few times and it just isn't going to happen like that. You see, I accepted this lady's offer to purchase this guitar—this is known as a binding legal contract. And I hereby proclaim under the laws of the great state of California that the guitar is mine," I said, hoping to appeal to both people's sense of patriotism and legal duty. At the same time, I tried to get Steve's attention to calm him down, because I just knew he was going to bid the guitar up in an attempt to torpedo my deal. If that happened, he was only going to enrich the seller, and one of the two guitar buyers was going to go home poorer. But it didn't work. Steve got ants in his pants and cast the first stone: "I'll give you $2,500 for it."

So at that moment I decided to make Steve pay and pay dearly. Since he was being a bad sport in the canon of guitar dealer ethics, I was going to bid the guitar up, and then at the last minute jump off that freight train, leaving him poorer and less able to compete with me on the next deal.

"I'll go $3,000."

He shot back, "$3,500."

"Four grand," I rejoined.

And so it went. I think we bid it up to $4,500 and then I smugly said, "Steve, it's all yours." Then came the realization that he would have to pay that much more in cash, and he became quite subdued. Now *he* was the one who didn't have enough cash on hand to complete the transaction.

So Steve now had to go home to get additional funds to pay for the guitar. As we left the jubilant seller's house, I said, "Steve, why didn't you just pull me aside and offer me a few bucks? I would have clammed up and walked away, and *you*, good sir, would have gotten the guitar for $2,000 less. We both would have been winners."

He said, "Well, I didn't think about that." The lady waved us a good-bye, bearing an ear-to-ear grin.

Steve later ended up becoming a friend and sold me some nice guitars along the way. He sold me a beautiful 1963 Stratocaster and gave me a really good deal on it— because I think he felt just a smidgen guilty about that Telecaster deal. But I was still unhappy with the seller, because she'd said, "We have a deal." In the world of vintage guitars, a deal is a deal—even if someone offers more after you have accepted an offer. There have been many times when I have sold a guitar and then have been offered more for it while I was awaiting payment. Of course, it's always tempting to take the higher price and make the quick buck, but in the long run you only hurt yourself in so doing.

The moral of the story? In these kinds of situations, besides making sure you have enough cash in pocket to start with, we guitar dealers should be looking out for each other.

12

MY GENERATION

One day in 1994, I got a call from a fellow in Fresno, right in the middle of farming country in California's fertile Central Valley. His name was Elmore Blatch.

"I've got a 1959 Les Paul T.V. Junior that I want to sell for $1,500," he informed me. "Bought it new in '59 after I got back from Koh-ree-a." It was, at the time, a very reasonable price.

"If it's what you say it is, Elmore," I replied, "I'm prepared to buy it from you." I jumped in my trusty van and drove down to get a look at what might prove to be a very sought-after instrument.

I arrived in a modest neighborhood and was met at the door by a nice older gentleman. Judging from his flattop haircut and the memorabilia in his house, he had spent considerable time in the service of our military. Elmore invited me to sit in the living room while he went to get the guitar. While I waited, a fellow suddenly emerged from the back room. He looked about thirty-five years old. From the tattoos festooning his body, I guessed he might have done a stretch in prison or had at least been running with the wrong crowd. I could see a family resemblance to the old man and assumed that this charming-looking character was his son.

"What are you doing here?" he asked me.

"I'm waiting for Elmore," I said. "He's showing me his guitar."

"Why is he showin' you the guitar?" he inquired with barely concealed hostility.

"I'm hoping to buy it from him," I replied, wondering if I should make a beeline for the door instead, the 1959 Les Paul notwithstanding.

"You aren't touchin' that guitar!" he barked. "That's my fuckin' guitar!" I realized I had stumbled into the middle of a spiteful family squabble. Damn, that put me in a tight spot!

Alerted by his son's soothing voice, Elmore emerged from the rear of the house. "Butch," he shouted back, "get the hell out of here. That ain't your guitar, and I got the right to sell it any time I want."

A pitched verbal battle ensued, and that song "Stuck in the Middle with You" came into my mind. As the argument got more heated I found myself wondering if they would actually come to blows, or worse. Maybe this fine upstanding young man would pull out a knife and stab his pop and then attack your humble narrator.

Eventually the yelling died down, but the old man's son refused to leave and just sat there at the kitchen table fuming, scowling at me with a look that could kill. I suddenly realized that I was shaking and that no guitar, no matter how rare, was worth dying for. Yes, it truly was *Clowns to the left of me, jokers to the right. . . ."*

"Listen, Butch," the old guy continued after a moment, attempting to defuse the situation, "that's my guitar and I have to sell it. I need the money, son."

"That's my goddamn guitar, old man," his son spat back. "You told me I could have it twenty years ago," and he slammed his fist down on the side table. An ashtray full of cigarette butts fell to the floor. The two eyed each other with venomous expressions and I braced myself for the full-on brawl to break out. The kid's face was red, veins popping out of his neck, and he was so threatening that I assumed his father would give in and tell me the Les Paul was not for sale. But instead Elmore turned to me and asked, "Have you got that fifteen hundred bucks?"

I nodded and he handed over the guitar. Inspecting it for a split second, I reached in my pocket and pulled out the wad of bills. The kid then started yelling again and they both stood up. I was now certain that it was going to come to blows. But Elmore counted the bills—and about every fifth bill he looked up to make sure his son had not advanced on him. All I wanted was to get the hell out of there, but I was also prepared to give Butch a kabong to the head with his father's guitar if it meant me getting out of there with my skin. After Elmore finished counting the money and put the whole pile deep into his pocket, I turned to his son.

"I'll give you my phone number, Butch," I told him, writing "867-5309" on a piece of paper. "If you get some cash together you can buy this guitar back from me whenever you want." My offer seemed to calm the situation, at least for a minute, but as I was walking out the door, he must have realized that the number I had given him was bogus, and he threw the paper right back in my face. I got out of that place faster than a scalded rabbit, made it to my van, and vanished in the jet stream of cars heading north on Interstate 5 back to San Francisco.

This particular experience was an exception that proved the rule. It was the only time I ever felt threatened while hunting for guitars on the road. But what I learned long ago was reinforced that day: that certain instruments have a real emotional connection within families. Sometimes those emotions boil to the surface at a moment's notice. Butch and Elmore Blatch obviously had "issues"—issues way beyond who owned that particular guitar. I promised myself that in the future I would do my best to stay out of such charged domestic conflicts, no matter what the potential payoff.

Watching this father and son go head to head was an object lesson that there is often a generation gap between those who bought their guitars in the 1940s, fifties, and sixties, and their progeny in the decades that followed. These are two distinct age groups, with very different formative experiences, identities, and values. There is some overlap, obviously, but I have consistently found tremendous differences in dealing with people from those two generations during my many years in the guitar business.

One of the main differences is what I call the "integrity gap." Over twenty years of buying vintage instruments, I found that those who came of age during World War II—the so-called greatest generation—seemed to want, with few exceptions, to make sure that both sides of a deal were happy with a sale, and to make sure that it was a fair and equitable transaction for both sides. Generally, these folks would be honest in their descriptions of guitars and understood the principle that I needed to buy the instrument at a price that would allow me to make a profit.

On the other hand, younger people—those of my generation and younger—often felt no qualms about misrepresenting the quality of the instrument they were trying to sell. They often did not seem to want anyone else to make a single penny. Of course, there are honest and unscrupulous characters on both sides of the generational divide, but there is also a general rule of thumb I see confirmed time and again: folks of a certain age who have seen the hard side of life and have sacrificed for their families or the greater good seem, in my modest estimation, to be more trustworthy and straightforward.

I have often been gratified and fascinated when I had the chance to connect with those who lived through the great upheavals of the World War II era. I enjoy just sitting with them and hearing their stories, and I believe they, in turn, are many times just grateful to have someone lend an ear. The sagas of their lives and of their guitars often intertwine. It is enlightening and entertaining to listen as they relive memories. Sometimes these stories are heartwarming. Just as often they are heartbreaking. Sometimes the tales are thrilling, and sometimes they are harrowing. Many I will never forget, and I count it as a privilege to be a living witness to their accounts of our common humanity.

Another reminder of this so-called generation gap occurred when I got a call from an elderly man named Tony living in Menlo Park, just south of San Francisco. Tony was responding to an ad I had placed in the *San Francisco Chronicle* seeking to buy old Martin guitars.

By my best guess, Tony must have been born about 1910. "I've got a 1927 000-45 Martin guitar," he told me over the phone. "I bought it in 1931 when I saw it in San Francisco, sitting in a store window for fifty dollars."

I made a trip down to Menlo Park to take a look at his guitar, which I immediately wanted to buy, but I could also tell from the look in Tony's eyes that he was wavering and felt ambivalent about parting with this beautiful instrument. I suggested he give me a call when he was ready. As I was getting ready to leave, he let me know that he had recently brought the guitar to a local Martin dealer and that he had become suspicious after he was offered a meager $300 for it.

"I said no," Tony declared. "I told them I needed to think about it. Then, as I was walking out of the store, they up and offered me $500. Before it was all over they were putting $1,500 on the table. Right then I got angry and told them that when I'd walked in it had been worth just three hundred dollars. If they'd offered me $800 up front, I would have sold it, but I knew they were just trying to take advantage." Tony turned beet red as he recounted this story. He asked me to wait a year to call him again about the guitar.

So after a year I reconnected with Tony and told him that I still wanted to buy his Martin. He still wasn't quite ready, but I kept calling him and he finally relented.

"Okay," he told me at last, "I'm ready to sell. Come on down again and bring all your money!" That afternoon, before we got down to business, we talked about a whole range of subjects: politics, religion, culture, and art. I learned that Tony was from the Mediterranean island of Malta. He was a true gentleman.

"How much are you are going to sell me your Martin for?" I finally asked as the afternoon shadows lengthened through the curtained windows.

"How much are you offering?" he asked right back.

I knew I had to come up with something substantial in order to entice him to part with it. I proposed $10,000.

"I guessed it was only worth $5,000," he replied.

"No, Tony," I explained. "It is actually worth more than $10,000, but I have to make a profit on it. You have to admit my offer sure beats the $1,500 you were offered by the nice man at the guitar store."

He laughed, "Better than the $300 they first offered. Shoot, I would have taken $5,000 for it."

"Yeah?" I said, joining in his laughter, "It's never too late to lower your price!" With that, Tony at last parted with the guitar for $10,000—this was, after all, an instrument he had bought over a half-century earlier for fifty bucks. And I, in turn, was able to flip it for a very nice profit. Everyone was happy, except the storeowners who had attempted to lowball Tony. And to them the old adage applies: "Pigs get fat, hogs get slaughtered."

This story shows that a guitar sale can open up a retrospective window on an early and significant time in a person's life, especially if, like Tony, the owner is an older person who has had a guitar for many years. To him it might represent his youth and aspirations. Taking the time to listen to these folks, to establish a rapport, is instructive and invaluable—not just because they might trust you enough to pass on their guitar to the next owner, but sometimes an amazing story is just waiting to be told.

One World War II veteran told me how he had left his guitar with a friend at their infantry camp in the South Pacific when he went on a mission. On his return, he found that the camp had been attacked and his friend had been killed. But the guitar survived. Accounts such as his cut to the heart of who we are and why our mere physical possessions can sometimes have such powerful sentimental value. Yes, the reasons for selling a guitar are as varied as the people who sell them. Sometimes people need the money; sadly, I have met many folks who have no choice but to sell, even when it is the last thing they want to do. I have also met many a widow who has outlived her husband and has held onto the instrument her spouse once played as one of her most cherished possessions.

More than once I have had to try to offer comfort and solace to someone who has broken down when it came time to part ways with so precious an object. For these folks the sale can mean an era in their lives has come to a close. Yet, as that door closes, perhaps a new one is opening for the next owner of that guitar. After all, handing down important cultural items from one generation to the next is a tradition that a sophisticated society traditionally values. When a guitar goes from hand to hand, it can signify renewal, change, and redemption.

In obtaining an old guitar, one is buying the memories, both good and bad, that come along with it. Fortunately, the memories attached to a musical instrument are usually good ones. Sometimes when I buy a guitar it's hard to stop holding it, looking at it, and thinking, "If this guitar could only talk—the stories it might tell . . ." Holding a guitar that was made in the 1920s, before the Great Depression, it is hard not to think about the places that such an instrument has been, the people who have played it, the songs that have come forth from it, the owners who have cared for it. Sometimes you can just feel the energy and sense the spirits of the previous owners. For those of us who share a passion for such instruments—some of whom are dead and some still living—this business can get awfully sentimental.

13

GOEBEL REEVES: THE TEXAS DRIFTER

Every now and then a guitar drops into my lap, a guitar that somehow feels like an outright gift from heaven. Luck has always seemed to be on my side in these adventures, because when I needed it most, providence has dutifully intervened on my behalf. And in late October 2008, I was in a very tough spot financially, like the rest of the world. George Bush was about to leave office and ride into the sunset on his not-so-white Texas horse. The country was still at "war" in Iraq. The economy was sputtering at its worst since the Great Depression. The words "pessimism" and "malaise" seemed to sum up the times.

Yes, even the most steadfast Republicans were glum during this election cycle. And when I headed to Arizona on a guitar-buying voyage, I was shocked to see the lack of McCain/Palin signs and bumper stickers in the home state of the Republican nominee for president of the United States. I only saw one such sticker emblazoned on a car during the three days I was there. That said much to me about McCain's prospects on November 4, and ironically it said much about my prospects for acquiring guitars for resale on this trip. Sadly, the worse the economy, the better my prospects were for buying guitars on the cheap, and on this particular trip, the U.S. economy was beginning its most precipitous decline.

I dropped in to see a nice couple in Winslow, Arizona, who had called me about a Gretsch guitar they wanted to sell. It turned out it was a 1957 Gretsch Duo-Jet, jet-black and in very nice original condition. This guitar was nearly identical to the one George Harrison had played when he was with the Beatles. When I came to the Turners' home, it was clear that times were very difficult for these good folks. Joe had gone through years of serious illness.

The retired couple, perhaps in their early seventies, had to sell the Gretsch guitar just to get by. Since the market was very slow for vintage guitars at this time, I told myself that I could pay only half of what I usually would. So when I saw the beautiful Gretsch, I had to remain resolute to offer the Turners less than my customary good bid for that desirable guitar. They had little choice but to accept; sometimes capitalism is a harsh reality. It certainly didn't make it any easier to stomach when Joe started crying as I closed the case and he said goodbye to the cherished guitar he had owned since the 1950s. "So much for trickle-down economics," I murmured as I put the guitar in my van and drove back to my motel. Being conservative in this instance was the right thing to do. I could only sell that guitar for exactly what I had paid for it. And so, in the end, the only person who made money on the guitar was Joe.

The next day was going to be extraordinary and certainly more profitable. I had received a call from a man with a Fender Jazzmaster guitar. He thought the guitar was in original condition and proposed a price that made it worth the hour-and-a-half drive. But this fellow's abode was off the beaten path—literally; I found myself five miles off the highway on a dirt road, lost. By the time I made it to the guitar, I was just happy to stop. At least

I had escaped the punishment of that bumpy desert thorough-fare. I was disappointed to see the guitar; it had been refinished long ago, which diminished the value to such an extent that I could not buy it and make any profit. It was an innocent mistake on the behalf of the seller. Only an expert could have detected that the guitar had been refinished, but since that was the case, I decided to stay for a while and discuss music with the nice people who had invited me into their home. It is interesting to talk with people about their favorite songs, and we had many favorites in common, starting with Duane Eddy's 1958 seminal "Rebel Rouser."

Duane Eddy is considered by many to be the first guitar hero. Some would argue that the title should belong to Les Paul. Both were trailblazers of the early electric guitar days. I mentioned to my host that I owned a recording studio in California because he mentioned that his son was looking for a place to record. I gave him my business card and told him to have his son call me anytime to discuss music recording.

As I walked out the door, the fellow said, "Oh, by the way, do you buy old Martin guitars?"

I replied, "Yes, indeed . . . why? Do you have one?"

"No," he replied, "but I know an old man that lives back in the town of Winslow that you are going to; he has a 1936 Martin he might sell." And with that, his wife looked up Joe Aruda's telephone number in the phone book, wrote it on a scrap of pa-per, and gave it to me. I thanked them and drove my now filthy vehicle back to the glorious town of Winslow.

Winslow, Arizona, is a rather odd town. It is located off High-way 40 near the middle of Arizona. Commerce comes from the millions of eighteen-wheelers that pass through on the way to California from all over the nation. Disappointed so far in my search, I intended to get a good night's sleep in one of the many luxurious Motel 6 affairs that were my home away from home. I guess it says much about the state of things when you are keen to get back to the luxury of a Motel 6. By the way, I wish Motel 6 would quit leaving that damn light on for me. If they would just turn it off and save some electricity and lower the room rates, we would all be better off. Ya' hear me, Tom Bodett? But let's get back to Winslow . . .

When I arrived at my oasis in the desert, I decided to make a few final guitar calls before I turned on the television and wound down for the night. The third call I made was to Joe. Sure enough, Mr. Aruda answered the phone, though he was a little surprised by my call. "Who ya' say gave ya' my number?" It was obvious that Joe's hearing was not so good. But one thing was crystal clear: that he wanted $5,000 for his Martin guitar. He asked if I could afford a $5,000 Martin. I thought to myself, "Perhaps I can't afford *not* to have a $5,000 Martin."

From 1935 to 1940, the Martin guitar company had its golden era. This is when Martin had access to the finest first-growth Brazilian rosewood for the guitar bodies, the finest Sitka spruce for the top of the guitar, and the finest ebony and mahogany for the fingerboards and necks of the guitars. It was also when they had their best craftsmen. Moreover, like fine violins, these guitars have become better with age. The woods have cured, the glues have dried, and the nitrocellulose lacquer has mellowed, making Martin guitars from this era the finest in the 182 years that the company has been in business. So it was with obvious enthusiasm that I went to see Joe's guitar.

When I arrived, I noticed that Joe's house was a "double-wide," a euphemism for a trailer that is essentially a home on wheels. Joe informed me that he was selling his guitar because he hadn't played it for years and he needed the money. So we chatted for about forty-five minutes before he brought out the old Martin guitar. Joe told me of his life as a bus mechanic before he'd become a professional Ping-Pong player in the 1950s. He had spent much time in California and had even played Ping-Pong at San Quentin. Joe had apparently done a short stretch at that illustrious prison in Marin County, California, that looked out across the San Francisco Bay.

Being from a California family and having some fondness for Ping-Pong myself, I had much to talk about with Joe. Finally Joe asked me to open up the old guitar case that housed the '36 Martin. The first thing I noticed was the condition of the case itself. It had obviously seen better days, and I saw that the case had been repainted; this fact is usually significant. Someone who takes time to paint a guitar case usually has also taken time to refinish the guitar inside, and, as I mentioned earlier, a guitar that has been stripped or refinished loses value, usually to the tune of fifty percent or more. In fact, this is the way most guitars are devalued. So, as the old case creaked open, I suspected I would find a guitar that was not in prime collector's condition. I was wrong. Exceptionally wrong.

The guitar appeared to be a 000-45 model. Martin guitars are built on a size schedule and a materials and ornamentation schedule. Sizes range from the orchestra models (0 to 000) to the "dreadnought" (D) guitars, which are the largest of all Martins. Then comes the materials-and-ornament number, starting with 15 (mahogany with no ornaments) and progressing to 45 (rosewood and highly ornate). So this guitar appeared to be the largest orchestra model with the highest degree of ornament: the 000-45. The ornaments on one of these fancy Martins are substantial. They have mother-of-pearl inlays all around the body, on the headstock, and around the sound-hole.

In short, this guitar appeared to be one of the finest Martin guitar models ever produced. Moreover, such instruments are exceedingly rare. Martin made only 125 of these beautiful guitars between 1934 and 1943, when they were discontinued. My first thought was, *It can't be.* Joe told me that he had recently had the guitar appraised and that it was worth only $5,000. So my second thought was that this guitar was a 000-21 model that someone had added "after-market" ornamentation onto. A 000-21 from 1936 would be worth in the neighborhood of $5,000, so that seemed to make sense. Then I looked in the sound-hole and saw the serial number and the 000-45 stamped in the base of the neck. I wondered, "Could this be a bona fide original 000-45?" This was a tough call.

To make an accurate determination, I queried Joe about the guitar: Where had he gotten it? How long had he owned it? Had anyone done any repair work on it? Who had appraised it? The answers only muddied the water. Joe told me that he had been given the guitar some twenty-five years earlier by a member of his ministry, and that someone had done work on the guitar years before that. When I asked, "Did the guitar have the pearl ornaments when you received it twenty-five years ago?" Joe thought that they were original to the instrument, but he wasn't sure.

So I made a decision to purchase the guitar thinking that (worst case) the guitar was a 000-45 "conversion" that would be worth the $5,000 that I was going to pay for it. Much better was the possibility that the guitar was a genuine 1936 000-45 that was being sold to me at one-tenth its retail value. I was obviously hoping for the latter, but was expecting the former. Joe was perhaps finally tiring of the small talk when he said, "Well, what do ya' think?" I responded by saying I would purchase the guitar from him at his asking price. Joe seemed very happy that I had agreed to his proposal; I surmised that he either really needed the money or was eager to unload a converted guitar that was very difficult to sell.

So I reached into my pocket and remembered that I had spent some of my money on the hotel room and gas, and—shucks, maybe I didn't even have the five G's that old Joe wanted. So I counted out my money, emptying my pockets and my wallet. The result: $4,600. So I told Joe that I was $400 short. I suggested that he take the $4,600 and let me write him a check for $400. Joe squinted and looked at me and kindly replied, "I said $5,000 cash, boy. That means five thousand in cash—I don't take no checks."

Seems like a little bit of that anger that probably got Joe locked up in Quentin in the first place was boiling to the surface. Now the old Ping-Pong hustler had me on the ropes. "Well, I do believe that I can go to the ATM and get four hundred more dollars."

"Fine," he grunted, "I ain't goin' nowhere."

I asked if I should leave him a deposit and he said, "Nope."

I began to believe he really was not so eager to sell the guitar, and this suggested that it might in fact be an original 000-45. So I told Joe that I would be back as soon as I could find a Wells Fargo bank.

I got into my van and hightailed it across town. When I found the local Wells Fargo, I was only able to take out $100 because I had already withdrawn $200 that day; the limit was $300 per day. So now paranoia set in: "I'm probably going to lose a once-in-a-lifetime guitar over $300," I thought to myself. I desperately called several of my friends, hoping to get someone to Western Union me three hundred measly dollars.

Finally, I reached a business colleague at 7:30 p.m. He agreed to wire me the money, but by the time I had gone to three Western Union offices to get the money, it was eleven o'clock—far too late to go back and see Joe. I would just have to wait until morning. But this got my wheels turning: what if Joe had called the guy who had appraised the guitar and asked him if he could get more money from someone else? Worse, what if the appraiser had given Joe a lowball appraisal with hopes of someday buying the guitar from him on the cheap? These thoughts were bad enough, but when I got back to my hotel room and looked up the value of this guitar in the current *Vintage Guitar Price Guide*, I was astounded: $90,000 to $115,000. Safe to say it was a very long night.

All this paranoia was for naught. I was there bright and early and the obviously volatile Mr. Aruda had the guitar waiting for me on the couch. I gave him the money, thanked him, and took the guitar back to my hotel room to examine it to see if it was the real deal or a "frugase," as they would say in New York. My preliminary examination suggested that the guitar was indeed an original 000-45 Martin, but I did not have the proper tools to look inside the guitar to be certain. Odds now were pretty good I had hit the proverbial home run. Then I noticed something on the guitar case. It looked as if someone had painted some words on the case, perhaps long ago—a common thing for musicians in the old days to do. But since the guitar case had been painted over, I couldn't quite make out the words. I could see what appeared to be a star.

So, after my long trip home, I quickly took the guitar to my friendly local guitar repairman and resident Martin expert to have the instrument evaluated. I was thrilled to learn that the guitar was a fully original 1936 000-45 Martin, one of the holy grails of the guitar world. It had been quite some time since I had made a find of this caliber—but it was to get better yet!

When I took some denatured alcohol and rubbed it on the illegible writing on the guitar case, it came into clear view that the lettering spelled "Texas Drifter." This moniker sounded vaguely familiar, but I could not recall who might have used it. I quickly went to my potent research tool, the Internet, and googled "Texas Drifter." Instantly it became clear who the former owner of this exquisite instrument was . . . and it all started to make sense.

Goebel Reeves was a singer/songwriter who left middle-class life to become a vagabond, earning a living as a traveling singer after he was wounded in World War I. He called himself the "Texas Drifter," and the name stuck. Goebel wrote one of Woody Guthrie's signature tunes, "Hobo's Lullaby," in the early 1930s. And, according to legend and his own claims, he taught Jimmie Rodgers to yodel. An interesting point regarding the 000-45 Martin is that Jimmie Rodgers also played a 000-45 (1928 model). Reeves and Rodgers are known to have traveled and performed together in the early 1920s. Reeves' recording debut was on OKeh records in 1929. Through the 1930s Reeves cut about thirty-five sides for various labels; they followed the Rodgers mold in their mix of freedom-of-the-road yodeling numbers, comic pieces (such as a mother-in-law-joke parody of "St. James Infirmary"), and sentimental ballads. But Reeves specialized in reflective hobo-philosopher recitations that were quite distinct from Rodgers' hobo pieces. He composed virtually all of his own recorded material. Reeves also made his singing and guitar-playing debut on the silver screen in the movie *Silver Trail* in 1937. His last recordings were in 1938 for a radio-transcription company in Hollywood.

Occasionally Reeves appeared on radio in both the U.S. and Canada, doing brief stints on the *Rudy Vallee Show, National Barn Dance*, and the *Grand Ole Opry*. Later in the thirties, he returned to his seafaring career and spent time in Japan. During World War II, he entertained U.S. troops and then, because he spoke some Japanese, worked for the U.S. government in Japanese-American internment camps. Reeves died in a veterans' hospital in Long Beach, California, in 1959. Several LP reissues in the 1970s reintroduced the almost-forgotten Reeves to country music fans, and his complete studio recordings were collected on the 1994 Bear Family release *Hobo's Lullaby*.

Several modern country artists have covered Goebel Reeves songs, including Arlo Guthrie and Emmylou Harris, who both sing a beautiful rendition of "Hobo's Lullaby." When I held this guitar, I appreciated it as more than just a singular example of Martin guitar craftsmanship. It is the heirloom of a true individual musician: an unsung yet important part of America's musical heritage. What a find.

14

NEMO DAT QUI NON HABET
(HE WHO HATH NOT CANNOT GIVE)

O ne of the musicians who had the biggest influence on my early aspirations to pick up a guitar was Ronnie Montrose, who remains one of my all-time favorite players.

In 1968, as a twenty-one-year-old guitar slinger, Ronnie came from Colorado to San Francisco, the center of all things musical at the time, to hone his craft. He first started his own band, called Sawbuck, but soon moved on to back up Van Morrison, just when the singer's career was taking off. The guitar parts on the classic "Wild Night" are some of the finest early guitar riffs that Ronnie Montrose lent to Mr. Morrison's exquisite breakthrough album, *Tupelo Honey.*

Not long after this dazzling debut, Ronnie was picked up to perform on the Edgar Winter Group's smash album *They Only Come Out at Night.* Released on Epic Records in 1972, the album helped establish Ronnie's growing reputation for innovation, exemplified by such enduring rock anthems as "Frankenstein" and "Free Ride."

A year later, Ronnie broke ranks with Edgar's group and struck out to form a new band of his own. Not long after, a young singer by the name of Sammy Hagar knocked on Ronnie's door in Sausalito, California. Hagar was eager to work with the guitar virtuoso after being profoundly impressed by Ronnie's performance at a Winterland appearance with the Edgar Winter Group on February 3, 1973.

With drummer Denny Carmassi and bass player Bill Church, they formed the rock group Montrose, and their 1973 debut album, also titled simply *Montrose*, is still widely considered one of the greatest hard rock albums ever recorded. It was not long after that *Guitar Player* magazine rated Ronnie Montrose one of the top two guitar players in the world (Jimmy Page was rated number one).

Sammy Hagar stayed with Montrose to sing on the follow-up album (*Paper Money*) before departing to start his own band. In 1977, the rock band Van Halen, who had been playing Montrose cover songs as part of their repertoire when they were just another club band on the Hollywood music scene, were signed by Montrose producer Ted Templeton to the Warner Brothers Records label. It is no coincidence that Warner Brothers signed Van Halen, since it was the band's stated goal "to sound like Montrose."

There is no question that both Ronnie and his band Montrose helped to write an influential chapter in rock 'n' roll history. Ronnie expanded the expressive potential of the hard rock electric guitar. With his 1958 Fender Bandmaster amplifier and his 1958 Les Paul Standard Sunburst guitar, he singlehandedly raised the bar on how rock music tonality could become much heavier and much more saturated.

I first met Ronnie Montrose in 1980, when I dropped by a San Francisco music store called Satterlee & Chapin to show the owner my latest 1958 Gibson Les Paul Standard guitar. As mentioned earlier, the original model Les Paul Standard Sunburst guitars were made from 1958 to 1960. After 1960, Gibson radically redesigned the body style of the Les Paul, creating a wholly different shape for the venerable bestseller. This new shape was shunned by the guitarists of the early and mid-1960s, and as a result the earlier Les Paul model became coveted. This was especially so after guitarists such as Michael Bloomfield, Eric Clapton, Jeff Beck, Jimmy Page, Peter Green, Keith Richards, and George Harrison appeared on stage with the older, original editions of the Les Paul. To be precise, the guitars used by these stars tended to be Les Paul Standards manufactured in 1958, 1959, or 1960. These instruments, because of the distinctive stained "sunburst" finish on their maple wood face, were nicknamed "Sunbursts."

Sunburst Les Pauls from the 1950s are sometimes given an individual name—either a moniker for that instrument's particular wood-grain, or perhaps the name of a prominent former owner. A friend of mine once owned the "Marin Burst," one of the great Sunburst Les Paul guitars that I made the mistake of not buying. The instrument was named for its long history in Marin County, California. This practice of naming an instrument is borrowed from the Stradivarius violin community. Often the illustrious seventeenth- and early eighteenth-century violins were given a sobriquet, or nickname.

The original Les Paul guitars became the instrument that aficionados consider equal to the legendary Stradivarius violin as the standard of excellence. Small wonder that when Ronnie Montrose saw the telltale case of my '58 Les Paul in the music store that day, he knew exactly what was inside.

"So what year is your Sunburst?" he asked, by way of introducing himself.

I was a little nervous, with good reason. This was the first time I had ever met a celebrity musician, much less one of my musical heroes.

"It's a '58," I managed to blurt out.

"Can I see it?" Ronnie asked, and I remember thinking how shy and unassuming he seemed. He was showing keen interest, which was not surprising; he was known to own several of these guitars, and I had seen pictures in guitar magazines of him performing on various Sunbursts. I put the case down, opened it, and was struck by the approval on Ronnie's face when he saw what was inside.

"Damn," he said. "That's a nice one. It kind of reminds me of the '58 that I bought not long ago." I asked Ronnie how many Sunbursts he had in his arsenal.

"I've had three," he replied with a trace of regret. "I sold one and one was stolen. I only have one left."

Ronnie went on to explain that the purloined Sunburst had been stolen from him while he was playing a concert in Dudley, Massachusetts, in 1972.

"I put the guitar down on a stand," he said, "played a song with a bass guitar, and then came back to get my Les Paul. The only thing that was left was the strap draped over the stand."

I gave a low groan. "That sucks," I said. The coveted guitar had been stolen right off the stage. Then I had an idea. "I'm an active guitar collector," I told Ronnie. "If you can get me a photograph of that guitar, I'll keep my eyes open for it. Maybe I can help you find it."

"I'm not sure I have a picture of it," he replied, "but let me look for one. I would sure appreciate any help you could give me to get that guitar back; I really miss it."

I gave Ronnie my phone number and was about to shake his hand and say good-bye when he made my heart jump by picking up my Sunburst and brandishing it over his head as if he was going to smash the guitar, à la Pete Townshend. Then he flashed a toothy grin and carefully lowered it back into its case. Thanks!

Mark Kremer, the gentleman who sold the 1958 Explorer and took a beating for it. (Photo courtesy of Mark Kremer)

The 1958 Gibson Explorer guitar that I purchased from Mark Kremer, serial number 8 3842. Atomic-age design sensibilities in full swing. I wish I had this one back! (Author's collection)

ABOVE: Gibson Super 400 CESN, 1957, unused condition—a veritable time capsule. I purchased this guitar in Redding, California, from the original owner. It had a case cover and still had the original wrapping paper inside the case. (Author's collection)

LEFT: A view of the 1957 Gibson Super 400 CESN, showing detail of the curly maple back. (Author's collection)

Guitar case for Goebel Reeves' 1936 Martin 000-45 guitar. I bought this guitar not knowing if it was a fake or a treasure. Fortunately, it was the latter. The case was spray-painted black, and when I removed the paint, the words "Texas Drifter" became visible. (Photo by Laura Kudritzki, courtesy of Laura Kudritzki Photography)

ABOVE: 1936 Martin 000-45. This guitar sounds even better than it looks. (Photo by Laura Kudritzki, courtesy of Laura Kudritzki Photography)

INSET: 1936 Martin 000-45 headstock detail. (Photo by Laura Kudritzki, courtesy of Laura Kudritzki Photography)

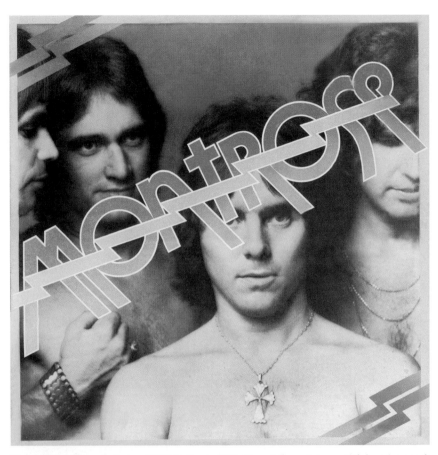

The band Montrose's first, self-titled album, 1973. One of the quintessential American rock and roll albums, one that changed the course of rock history. (Author's collection)

Edgar Winter and Ronnie Montrose on August 22, 1972, Gaelic Park, Riverdale, Bronx, New York. This concert photo shows Mr. Montrose playing his 1959 Les Paul less than two months before it was stolen. (Photo by Bob Solberg)

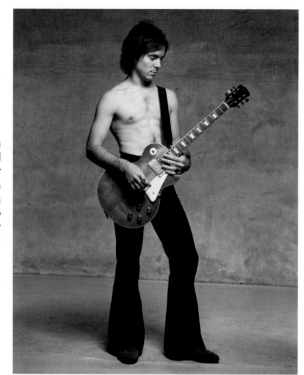

Ronnie Montrose with 1959 Gibson Les Paul Standard, serial number 9 2227, photographed in 1972 by famed fashion photographer Francesco Scavullo. (Photo by Francesco Scavullo)

Gary Moore holding the 1959 Gibson Les Paul Standard, serial number 9 2227, Ronnie Montrose's stolen guitar. (Photo by Sam Scott-Hunter)

Postcard from Van Horn, Texas. This is the town where Mike Parker and I found a wonderful stash of unused vintage guitars and amps. The following year, Jay Rosen and I were almost ambushed by a young woman that lived at the same residence. Yee-ha! (Photo by John "Daddy O" Payne)

Duke Wander, Georgia's husband, circa 1955, with the 1954 Gibson ES 350 guitar that was eventually given as a gift to Paul McCartney. (Photo courtesy of Georgia Wander)

Sir Paul McCartney and me at the Staples Center in Los Angeles on November 30, 2005. (Paul McCartney staff photographer)

That encounter marked the beginning of my friendship with Ronnie. Thereafter, with characteristic generosity, he helped me further my musical goals, and even taught me many of his guitar chops. In return, I helped him with his vintage guitar and amplifier needs. In 1995, we started the Big Industries amplifier company together. Ronnie had designed a superb little battery-powered amp we called the Ronnie Montrose Signature Model. At the N.A.M.M. trade show in 1995, we had initial orders for over eleven hundred units in our first weekend. We couldn't build them fast enough. Our success effectively put us out of business, since we had not anticipated such overwhelming demand.

A few years after our Big Industries venture, I began employing the Internet in the search for Ronnie's stolen Sunburst. Our first step was to appeal directly to fans for photographs of the stolen guitar, since Ronnie had not been able to locate one in his own files. Eventually, we received an e-mail from a fan who said he had a picture of Ronnie playing the stolen Les Paul.

When we got a look at the vintage photo, it was clear that it was not going to be of much help to our detective work. It was a very good picture of Ronnie on stage with Edgar Winter in 1972, playing the Les Paul just before it was stolen, but the photographer was not close enough to the stage to capture the face of the guitar in sufficient detail.

Without that, we were back to square one. The top or "face" of the Les Paul guitar body, as it is known in guitar collecting, is the most identifiable and distinctive part of the guitar. It is made exclusively out of curly American maple, with a unique grain pattern known as "flame" or "fiddleback." It is as foolproof a form of identification as a fingerprint. No two are exactly alike.

If we had been able to get a good, close-up shot of the face of the guitar, I would have known exactly what to look for. Then, if I saw the instrument at a guitar show, in a catalog, or in a book,

I could track it for Ronnie and he could try to retrieve it. The photo we received, while certainly historic, was not enough. We needed a definitive picture and there was nothing left to do but hope—and wait for one to emerge.

That critical clue finally came later and arrived from a most unlikely source. An ex-girlfriend, who had not spoken with Ronnie since they had broken up years before, heard of our search and got in touch. She had found a picture she thought might help.

To our surprise and amazement, the photo was not only a beautiful portrait of Ronnie taken by the famed fashion photographer Francesco Scavullo, but also highlighted a close-up of Ronnie holding the stolen Les Paul. It was a perfect frontal shot, showing the pattern in the guitar's maple top in great detail. I knew definitively that I would be able to identify the guitar if I were ever to cross paths with it.

With a copy of the revealing photograph at my side, I spent hours examining every book, magazine, photograph, and catalog I could find that contained a photo of a Gibson Les Paul Standard guitar from 1958 to 1960.

Amazingly, I found what I believed to be a match. It was exciting—like solving a riddle that had been posed twenty-five years before: what ever happened to Ronnie Montrose's stolen guitar? But there were big problems that came along with the possible discovery. It turned out that the guitar was rumored to be possessed by another rock star, Gary Moore, who resided in England. If it ever came to legal action, the Les Paul and its new owner were effectively outside of the jurisdiction of American courts and police.

"Now what the hell are we going to do?" Ronnie asked, with understandable frustration; we were so close and yet so far— clear across the Atlantic, to be exact.

Not to worry, I told him. I had studied law in England and was familiar with the country's civil common law and statutes. British law is very similar to United States law when it comes to stolen property. It stipulates that a person whose property is stolen never loses title to that property. In short, no matter how many years pass after a theft, the property remains that of the original, lawful owner or his or her heirs. No matter how many hands it has passed through or how much has been paid for it, even if the current or interim owners bought the property in good faith, the legal ownership of the property remains that of the deprived owner. Moreover, Ronnie had widely publicized his loss of the guitar and actively pursued its return. Before it was all over, Ronnie told me, "I even hired a private investigator in 1977, and he charged me a fortune to try to get the damn guitar back. Even he couldn't find it!" Ronnie would spend nearly three times the value of the guitar in 1972 dollars trying to track it down (he had purchased the Sunburst from Boston rocker J. Geils for $750 in 1972).

Ronnie called his longtime lawyer, Robert Gordon, to whom he had entrusted his entire professional career, authorizing him to give me access to the private investigator's reports from years before. Mr. Gordon had kept everything pertaining to the theft of the guitar and forwarded his entire file to me. Inside, the investigation was laid out in fascinating detail. From the reports I learned that Ronnie had been alerted, sometime after the theft, that a Massachusetts man named Gene Gagliardi knew the whereabouts of the guitar.

Gagliardi had sent a letter to Rick Derringer, who replaced Ronnie in Edgar Winter's band in 1973. In very cryptic terms he said in this letter that he knew who had the guitar and that the thief was racked with guilt about having stolen it. Eventually, the private eye became certain that Gagliardi had possession of the instrument. He placed this prime suspect under surveillance, but was never able to determine the location of the missing Les Paul. Ronnie stopped the investigation at the end of 1977. In 1995, when we were alerted that Gary Moore might have purchased the stolen guitar, we had one very big problem: we had no solid evidence that Mr. Moore currently had possession of the instrument. I attempted to contact Gary Moore's management and also tracked down the telephone number of Gary's guitar tech in an attempt to verify whether Gary Moore had the stolen guitar. My inquiries were received without a reply. So the trail went cold again. How would we ever find this guitar?

In 2007, some thirty-five years after the guitar was stolen, the search resumed after a friend sent me a copy of a British guitar magazine that featured the guitar collection of Gary Moore. Prominently included in this article were pictures of Ronnie's stolen 1959 Les Paul Standard guitar, serial number 9 2227. We eventually succeeded where the detective had failed in pinpointing the possessor of the Sunburst: Gary Moore. Moore claimed to have used the guitar on his hit song "Still Got the Blues." I quickly contacted a college buddy who had become an attorney, told him the story, and learned that one of the partners in his firm had litigated a similar case in the mid-nineties.

In that situation, a Stradivarius violin had mistakenly been left on the top of a car by a member of UCLA's Roth String Quartet, who had been loaned the violin. The priceless violin fell off the roof somewhere on the highway in Los Angeles. Twenty-seven years passed before it turned up again, when the Stradivarius was brought into a violin shop in Petaluma, California, to be repaired. The owner of the shop recognized it as the infamous lost UCLA violin and confronted the "owner," who claimed that she had been gifted the violin in good faith and that it was now *her* property. UCLA brought legal action and eventually prevailed in a landmark case that made the front page of the *New York Times*.

Unfortunately, the stolen Montrose Les Paul was a different matter. There were complex international jurisdictional issues involved. Since an American court could not compel a U.K. citizen to return the stolen property to its rightful owner, Ronnie had to be patient. Sooner or later, Moore, who was an actively touring musician, might return to the United States to perform. If he brought the guitar with him, it could be seized under a writ of possession.

Moore never did return to the U.S. with the Sunburst. Finally, Ronnie decided he should go to England to get that guitar back. The plan was simple: Ronnie would first approach Gary Moore, musician to musician, and ask for the return of his guitar. He hoped that if he could prove to the English guitarist with compelling evidence that he was in possession of Ronnie's stolen guitar, he would return it. But when Mr. Montrose sent a heartfelt letter to Gary Moore, laying out the history of the theft and politely asking for its return, we heard nothing from Mr. Moore. And this led us thereafter to file a lawsuit in U.S. District Court in San Francisco to sue for the return of Ronnie's stolen guitar.

One of the high hurdles we would have to meet in that legal action was to show that Gary Moore had ongoing "minimum contacts" with the San Francisco jurisdiction. The federal court ruled against us on this point, which meant that any further legal action would need to happen in the United Kingdom. Not only would this have required Ronnie to hire legal representation in the U.K., but also he would likely have had to travel there to prosecute this lawsuit. And although he was determined to right a wrong that had been perpetrated thirty-plus years before at a concert in Dudley, Massachusetts, Gary Moore's untimely death in February 2011 seemed to dash any further hopes of getting the instrument quickly returned to the hands of its rightful owner. Although Ronnie was himself ill at the time, as soon as his health improved, we were going to continue the efforts to see that his stolen guitar was returned. Ronnie was not a quitter.

Then, on March 3, 2012, as I was crossing the Golden Gate Bridge as a passenger in a car, I saw something amazing. Since I am usually the one driving, it was one of the few times I crossed the bridge and was able to look outward from the golden shore to the Pacific Ocean. Halfway across the bridge, I witnessed the very moment that the sun set on the ocean's horizon. This was the first time I had witnessed this: a small poof of emerald green flashed just as the sun disappeared from view. A few minutes later I learned that my dearest friend of thirty-two years, Mr. Ronnie Montrose himself, had passed away on that beautiful San Francisco afternoon. Ronnie would not live to see the day that his treasured guitar would be returned to him.

Just a few months earlier, Ronnie's beloved wife Leighsa had put together a sixty-fourth birthday party for Ronnie at Wolfgang's Vault, the home of the Bill Graham archives in San Francisco. The party, which was comprised of his closest friends and family, was, according to Ronnie, "the happiest day of my life." Ronnie was treated to a sing-along of the famous Beatles song "When I'm Sixty-Four" by the entire party.

Since that day when I met Ronnie in 1980, he had become at once a musical mentor, best friend, and a big brother. Not many people can say that their childhood hero became their best friend. What a blessing it was to have known him.

And now there is a new effort to see that Ronnie's Les Paul is returned to his lawful heirs. The long twilight battle is far from over. Stay tuned.

15

LAST TANGO IN VAN HORN

Earlier in this book I shared one of my favorite stories: the discovery of a cache of vintage guitars in Van Horn, Texas, in 1992. The find was the unexpected outcome of my efforts to rattle Mike Parker, friend and fellow road warrior, by showing him my genius "secret method" of finding great guitars.

A year after that unlikely happenstance, I headed back to the Texas Guitar Show with another collecting colleague and dear friend, Jay "the Hasidic Hammer" Rosen. As we drove, I regaled Jay with what had happened to Mike and me on the same road trip a year earlier.

"Let's go back," Jay said enthusiastically after I finished my tale. "I'd love to see that place for myself—and who knows? Maybe there are still some guitars in that old store."

After two dusty days of driving, it seemed a good idea to take a break, so we turned off the interstate. When we arrived in Van Horn, I headed straight for the run-down old building where we had first found Frank, the old man who owned the music store and had hung onto a pile of collectible amps and guitars behind its paper-covered windows. Sure enough, the building was just as we had left it. But this time, when we went upstairs and knocked, instead of a crusty old-timer an attractive young woman greeted us.

"Hi," she said cheerily, in an accent only slightly less thick than molasses in winter. "Can I help y'all?"

"Hi! I'm one of the guys who bought some guitars from an older gentleman here last year," I explained.

"Yeah, that was my *abuelo*," the girl replied. "He still has some of them thar' geetars down thar'. If y'all want to take a peek, he'll be back in 'bout an hour or so."

I suggested that we might get a bite to eat and come back when her grandfather had returned.

"Can I hang with y'all?" she asked.

"Sure," I said. "Why not?" What single red-blooded male wouldn't want to span some quality time with an alluring señorita?

As we all climbed in the van and headed down the street to a Mexican restaurant, she noticed the racks of guitars in back. "Where you boys headin' with all these gee-tars?"

"We're collectors," explained Jay, "and we're going to a guitar show in Dallas."

"Oh, man," she replied. "Ya' know, if y'all fellas is interested in geetars, I got a friend with an old one he's had for a long time. He might even sell it to y'all. I could take ya' over there if y'all want."

Jay and I looked at each other with raised eyebrows and exchanged a simple nod. "Let's go." Our new friend kept looking back at the guitars.

Following her directions, we left town and drove a few miles until we reached a dirt road. That led us straight to a surreal scene that one might expect in a David Lynch film. A barren stretch of cactus badlands dotted with longhorn cattle and crisscrossed by roadrunners was all that was visible for miles. In the midst of this desolate wasteland was a dilapidated old shack that appeared little more than an adobe-style chicken coop. A large northern mockingbird squawked from its perch on a barbed wire fence as we walked to the open door.

Inside, the hovel was even more, shall we say, picturesque. A pit at least two feet deep had been dug in the middle of the earthen floor, where a couple of mangy mutts slept. Our guide introduced us to the two occupants of the house: a pair of characters who would have given Sailor and Bobby Peru from the Lynch movie *Wild at Heart* a run for their money.

These toothless Southern gentlemen, with faces like worn boot leather, perched in swayback recliners and seemed to be relaxing after what I guessed was a leisurely morning getting hopped up on crack cocaine. They barely acknowledged our arrival, staring into space and mumbling to each other instead.

Jay and I exchanged a look of utter disbelief, as if asking each other the same question at the same time: "What the hell are we doing here?" We had never seen anything like these two refugees from a Southern Gothic potboiler and we had to restrain ourselves to keep from laughing at our situation.

"Can I show these fellas your gee-tar?" the girl asked one of the hombres.

"Why not?" he answered in a deep, gravelly drawl.

Digging through the debris, she produced a cheap knock-off acoustic hardly worth the wood it was made from. The owner, meanwhile, seemed to be completely preoccupied with the sight of his own bare feet elevated above the dirt floor.

"Where ya' from?" his partner asked at last.

"'Frisco," I replied. "We're just passing through."

"Yeah," Jay whispered in my ear, "passing through with $300,000 worth of guitars out in the van."

"Maybe we ought to be getting back on the road," I said, but the girl who'd brought us had other ideas.

"Why don't y'all stick around and party with us?" she implored. "We don't get many visitors out here." She tapped her arm several times, intimating that some intravenous drugs were going to be an integral part of the festivities.

"No," I insisted, "We really appreciate your hospitality but need to get back out on the road again."

We bid a Texas-sized goodbye to the two gents and headed back to town.

"Y'all don't need to be in such a hurry," the girl said as we drove along the dirt road, kicking up clouds of dust. "I got another friend who's got a gee-tar, too—an even better one."

"That's hard to imagine," I crackled under my breath.

"Look," she said, leaning in close. "Why don't ya' fellas take me along with ya'? I won't be no trouble, I promise. I've always wanted to go to Cali."

"I don't know if that's such a good idea," I said. "I'll tell you what. Let's have some lunch like we were planning and we'll drop you back home on our way out."

"Good idea," Jay agreed quickly. Like me, he was getting fed up with this sham guitar hunt. And who knew where we would end up?

"By the way, I'm starving, Mike. And we really need to make some time before the day is done," Jay added.

Back in town we parked outside the San Remo Café, a genuine Mexican burrito joint, but our new friend seemed reluctant to leave the van. Jay stepped out first and turned to help the young lady onto the sidewalk.

"I'm hangin' with ya' friend," she told him. "Maybe he and I can have some fun." I was distracted for a moment and did not hear this exchange, but there was no missing the smarmy leer on Jay's face when I turned around. He later told me that the energetic young lady had let it be known she intended to perform a lewd act on your unassuming narrator.

Under other circumstances I might have been more obliging, but I suspected after the afternoon's runaround that she was up to no good. It was an impression confirmed when she started coming at me with a sinister gleam in her eyes. I was not sure whether she was going to tear my clothes off, steal my keys, or attempt to throw me out the door and make off in the van. Something unsavory was definitely in the works.

I tried to fend her off as she got closer, but it was not until I yelled, "Get the f#@& out of here!" and started beeping the horn that she finally backed off and climbed out the door. Jay came high-stepping back to the van and we squealed out of Dodge, leaving the consternated chica behind. A middle-finger salute was her way of saying goodbye.

The best we could surmise, she was trying to get us into a compromising position and then take any opportunity that presented itself to steal our van and guitars and leave us stranded in the desert. And it was only at that moment that I recalled the warning that Mr. Snark from the hardware store had given me a year earlier about the "nutty" granddaughter of old Frank. It must have been her.

"Jesus! We gotta get out of this place," I exclaimed, my heart beating rapidly.

"One thing's for sure," Jay said as Van Horn disappeared in our rear view mirror. "We're not in Kansas anymore." We started laughing at the sheer absurdity of our adventure and did not stop for many miles down the broad Texas highway. The crazy interlude reminded me again of all those guitars stashed under the tarps in the deserted music store.

And on the Fourth of July, some fifteen years later, I found myself back in Van Horn for a third time. More than anything, I was curious. Was Frank the old-timer still there? Had the crazy granddaughter gotten the deed to the ranch? I knew the chance of the music store owner being alive was not good, since he was probably pushing seventy-five the first time I saw him. But I could not resist the lure of that peculiar old place. So I rolled down the long two-lane road into Van Horn one more time and parked in front of the two-story building, keeping an eye out for any stray Texas belle with grand larceny or lewd vagrancy on her mind.

I was a little tense as I climbed the stairs to the residence for what would likely be the last time. And I almost jumped out of my skin when a clutch of pigeons flew out an open window. I knocked softly on the door—twice, then hard, three times— but there was no answer. Turning the unlocked door handle, I slowly pushed my way inside.

"Anybody home?" I called out. There was no answer. I looked around. Inside, the place was completely defunct; beer cans were everywhere and there was a dangerous hole in the floor one could have fallen through. I went back downstairs and jolted open the front door to where the music store had been years before. If my first impression of the store had brought to mind a Texas twister, it looked as if another, even more destructive cyclone had paid a visit. And the place smelled worse. There was still a mountain of junk, but no sign of any of the musical instruments.

On closer examination I came across some old canceled bank notes and checks under the name of Frank Rodriguez, the old Texan himself. There were also a few old sets of guitar strings, some music stands, and instruction books. But that was about it. As far as guitars go, someone had beaten me a long time ago to what was left.

What I found most striking was that, while time had had its way with that old building, it had acted even more ruthlessly upon the people I had seen there—people whose lives intersected mine in some strange and unforgettable ways.

Old Frank Rodriguez, for instance, had obviously long since gone to the other side. So too had my friend Mike "the Bug" Parker, who had accompanied me on my first trip here. Mike passed away in 2002 of natural causes, aged fifty-two. I spoke to him on the telephone the very night he died. I also remember vividly that on the fateful trip in '92, Mike and I listened to the Clinton, Bush, and Perot presidential debates on the radio on the trip home. The trip back to San Francisco from Dallas was uneventful, and we had a good time. Mike was a good "guitar friend," and I miss him.

Since that trip, now over twenty years ago, Clinton had served eight years as U.S. president, erased the national budget deficit, brought peace and prosperity to America—and had almost been impeached before leaving office. In 2008, another Bush was in the White House and we were at war again, in Iraq. The deficit had soared, the economy was in near collapse, and the standing of America around the world was at its lowest ebb since the inception of the Republic.

And there I was, back in Van Horn one more time—still on the hunt for vintage guitars. The German philosopher Friedrich Nietzsche wrote about the "eternal recurrence of the same" in his novel *Thus Spoke Zarathustra*. I guess this proved that old Fred got his thesis right.

As I drove away from Van Horn, I turned around to take one last look, just as a beautiful rainbow appeared directly over the deserted building. Pulling to the shoulder, I took a photo and then went on my way. As I drove off, I noticed a sign on the Interstate that read: "Don't Mess with Texas."

Amen to that, I thought and tossed up a little prayer to get home safely and, if the gods were willing, to enjoy a few more years of doing what I loved best: hunting for old guitars.

16

THE TWAIN SHALL MEET

My dear friend and trusted assistant Robin Williams (not the comedian) is acquainted with a chap named Rusty Anderson. Rusty, for the past thirteen years, has served as Paul McCartney's chief guitar player. Naturally, Robin had an inside track for tickets and perks from pal Rusty when McCartney came to perform in Sacramento in 2005—and he invited me to come along to the concert.

"You think Rusty can get us backstage?" I asked hopefully when Robin told me about the upcoming event.

"Let me see what I can do," he promised. After a few calls he reported back: "We've got great seats for the show and Rusty got us a pair of backstage passes."

"Oh, my giddy! Maybe we'll get a chance to meet Paul," I enthused in a moment of wishful thinking. It was an idea Robin quickly quashed: "I wouldn't count on it," he cautioned, with a laugh.

The night of the concert I drove up to Sacramento, where I met Robin and his girlfriend at the massive venue. Together we went backstage into what is called the "green room," a waiting area for the artists, their families, and special guests. True to rumor, the McCartney green room was unusually well stocked with vegetarian hors d'oeuvres and fine French libations. Robin introduced me to Rusty Anderson for the first time. I made sure Rusty knew what a sterling musical talent I considered him. He, in turn, took me around to the other band members, all of who were friendly and welcoming.

Also in the green room was a gentleman named Mike Pinder, founder and keyboard player of the British band the Moody Blues. He, too, was very accommodating to a fan like me. I've loved the Moody Blues for as long as I can remember.

"I've heard about you," Mr. Pinder said as he introduced me to his wife and his son. I made an instant connection with Mr. Pinder, who now lives in California, and ended up chatting with him at length. I told him that "Nights in White Satin" was one of my favorite songs; every time I heard it, it brought me right back to 1972, when I was a young boy growing up in the San Francisco Bay Area. This was already turning out to be quite a night.

The backstage gathering was just winding down when an escort arrived to usher everyone from the green room to their seats in little groups of four and five. The show was about to begin, but Mike and I were oblivious, talking music as the room slowly emptied until there were only a few of us left. Finally, the escort arrived to lead us through the backstage maze into the auditorium.

"You know," Mike said as we made our way through the labyrinth of hallways, charged with anticipation, "I haven't seen Paul since 1969." It was true that Paul and Mike Pinder had been known to knock about regularly back in the good old days of Swinging London. "I've always hoped our paths would cross again, but I guess it's true what they say: 'never the twain shall meet.'"

A security guard suddenly appeared and ushered Mike, along with his family and me, down a long concrete corridor. He stopped us and pointed to a doorway further down the hall. Thinking it was the way to our seats, we marched up to it, only to see a sign on the door that read:

Paul McCartney
Dressing Room

Now, I have been a Beatles fan since the ripe old age of five, following their music and lives for five decades. As mentioned at the beginning of this book, my very first musical recollections are of the Fab Four; I fondly remember their debut on the *Ed Sullivan Show* and the day shortly thereafter when my mother brought home the first Beatles album with its iconic album cover. *Meet the Beatles* graced the record rack and stereo turntable in our living room for decades.

It is hard to overestimate the impact the Beatles had on America. They were a salve to the nation's shattered spirit after the assassination of John F. Kennedy and an important voice of reason during the divisive Vietnam War. They also pioneered hugely influential fashion trends, from the "pudding basin" haircuts of the early sixties to the brass band costumes they wore during the *Sgt. Pepper* era. They were far beyond musical icons—they were a catalyst for unprecedented changes in our culture and our consciousness. All four were phenomenal musicians, but as a band, they were unparalleled.

As I stood in front of that dressing room door, my mind reeled with a lifetime of Beatles memories. I vividly recalled my uncle giving me a set of Beatles bobblehead dolls when I was five. I remembered David Brewer, the first kid in town to get a copy of the single "Revolution." That automatically made him the coolest kid in the neighborhood. To this day, I've held the opinion that "Revolution" and "Hey Jude" may well be the two greatest rock songs ever written. It is true that both John and Paul are widely regarded as musical geniuses, but together with Ringo and George (equally regarded in the music community), it was just hard to believe that all that talent existed in one "great little band," as Sir Paul still calls it.

The memories just kept on coming even as, down the hall, we could hear the crowd howling for the show to begin. They weren't all good memories, either. Watching Monday night football in October 1980, I joined millions of others in disbelief when announcer Howard Cosell broke in with the report that John Lennon had been shot in New York City. According to the announcer, Lennon was still alive, but his condition was critical, and even then crowds were beginning to gather outside the hospital where he had been taken.

Fifteen minutes later, it was all over. One of the most talented and important artists of our time was gone—murdered by a deranged fan. Shock turned to tears, and tears to disbelief over his passing. "Horrified" was the word I remember coming from George Harrison, and that was exactly how I felt, along with millions whose lives had been changed by the four Liverpool lads. Without John Lennon the Beatles could never reunite, and the dreams of music lovers around the world were crushed. While it was a huge loss for our generation, I could scarcely imagine the enormity of the loss for the friends and family of John Lennon.

Eight years later, when I saw Paul McCartney perform a concert in Berkeley, California, he revealed to the audience a poignant anecdote about the time he'd proposed a lyric change in "Hey Jude" to John Lennon. "Don't you dare!" John had insisted. Paul went on to intimate that he was nearly moved to tears every time he sang that line of the magisterial song in concert.

These memories—and many more—rushed back as we stood in front of Paul's dressing room in that Sacramento stadium. Suddenly it swung open and there he was, Sir Paul McCartney, knighted by the British queen, crowned by an adoring public. He was preparing to go on stage, buttoning up his shirt like any mortal being. But when he saw Mike Pinder standing there, whom he hadn't seen in thirty-six years, he stopped, loudly exclaimed his amazement, and hugged his old friend from the golden days of British rock. They embraced for what seemed like a full minute.

Paul and Mike were already reliving the old days when Paul caught a glimpse of me watching in awe.

"And who might you be?" he asked in his familiar Liverpudlian lilt.

I swallowed hard. Suddenly my mouth was very dry. "Umm, hello. I'm Michael," was all I could get out. I am usually pretty calm and collected, even around the most famous of personages. But this was different; I was simply speechless with admiration. I just stared, my mind blank as Paul and Mike continued down memory lane. I could not think of anything to say until I happened to notice an acoustic Epiphone Texan guitar sitting a mere three feet from me—the same guitar on which Paul had written "Yesterday." I was about to point this out and, I freely admit, show off a little of my Beatles guitar knowledge, when a security guard approached to escort Paul to the stage. The magic moment was over before it began, and I was still reeling as we took our seats and the house lights dimmed. I was humbled to have met, however briefly, one of my all-time musical heroes. I suppose if I had had to choose one person out of the seven billion people living on Earth to have met, it would have been Sir Paul.

After the Sacramento show, McCartney and the band were scheduled to take a break before playing in Los Angeles two weeks later. I was so struck by this encounter with Paul that I decided to find a nice guitar to present to him as a gift. Robin suggested we call Rusty.

"Let me ask Paul what kind of guitar he'd like," Rusty responded, and a few days later he came back with a very specific request. "Paul was wondering about a left-handed Gibson from the fifties," Rusty told us. "He's looking for an arch-top jazz model, an electric."

This request was a tall order. The most difficult requirement came from the fact that Paul was a left-handed guitarist. That meant he needed an instrument manufactured in exactly the inverse of a standard guitar. Gibson made very few left-handed guitars, and even fewer of its top-of-the-line models, such as the 1950s arch-top Paul had singled out. Accordingly, his request was nearly impossible to accommodate.

As I searched through my guitar database for a suitable guitar for Sir Paul, I suddenly remembered Georgia, a lady in Southern California who had contacted me a few years earlier. Georgia's husband had died and he had left her a left-handed 1954 Gibson ES-350 guitar. She had even sent me a picture of the guitar. It was exactly what Paul was looking for.

The photograph of the guitar, taken in the mid-fifties, showed a dapper young man playing his left-handed Gibson. It was Georgia's husband, Duke, who was apparently no slouch when it came to entertaining. He had bought the guitar when it was new in 1954 and owned and played it over a period of almost fifty years. So I rang Georgia and asked if she wanted to part with the Gibson. The first time we had spoken, two years earlier, she was not yet ready to sell the instrument because she was contemplating leaving it to her son. This time, I planned to persist in my pitch, hoping that she would decide to let it go. But I only reached Georgia's answering machine, so I left a message.

For the next few days, I began pressing my guitar-dealer friends for an instrument they might have that fit the description of what Paul wanted. There were a few candidates, but nothing that quite measured up as a worthy gift for the former Beatle. Georgia, who had not called back, was quickly becoming my last resort.

The day before the McCartney concert in Los Angeles, Georgia finally called back.

"I have to tell you, Michael," she said, "I do think I'm interested in selling you the guitar."

When I asked Georgia about her change of heart, she told me her son had recently been killed in a car accident. I could understand her new willingness to let go of the instrument. She sadly had nobody to leave the guitar to now. But, even so, when she added, "I'm *almost* sure I'll be willing to sell it." I knew that her mind really wasn't fully made up.

After expressing my condolences for her loss, I apprised her of the situation. "Georgia, the only day I'm going to buy this guitar from you, and pay you full pop for it, would be tomorrow. That's when I'm going to see Paul McCartney in Los Angeles. I want to present it to him as a gift. Aside from that, I don't really have a lot of interest in buying it—unless it's at a wholesale price."

Letting her know this full-price opportunity was a one-time offer did the trick. Or perhaps it was the idea that the guitar was going to the most famous musician in the world that persuaded Georgia to sell. She was suddenly willing to make a deal. "Okay," Georgia said, "you come down here tomorrow morning, take a look at it, and make me a good offer. I'm sure we can work it out."

The next day I flew to the Ontario Airport, just east of Los Angeles, excited to finally get a look at an instrument that was as rare as hen's teeth. Georgia lived in Moreno Valley, a town near

Palm Springs at the edge of the desert. I pushed my rental car as fast as I could to get me there before she changed her mind. Moreover, I was running late—and had a strict deadline: Paul's concert was only hours away.

As I drove, I dialed Rusty's number to alert him of my projected arrival time at the concert.

"I've got your backstage passes all arranged," Rusty assured me. "Do you think you're going to have the guitar?" "I'll find out soon enough," I replied as I pulled up to the curb in front of Georgia's home.

Once I had a chance to talk directly with Georgia in person, I suspected she really was ready to let the instrument go. Like many of the people from whom I buy guitars, she just wanted to be sure her heirloom was going to the proverbial good home, and that the history of the guitar and its importance to her family would be passed along and respected by the new owner.

As I listened to Georgia, I was touched by the way tragedy had so quickly and repeatedly struck her life. Both her husband and her son had died within a short time of each other. As she talked about how much she missed them, I could see her beginning to waver on her promise to come to an agreement with me. In the end, I spent nearly three hours with the bereaved woman as she told me anecdote after anecdote before I finally asked her point-blank what she wanted. "Money—that's what I want!" was her witty reply. It was 4:00 p.m. when we consummated the deal and I hurried to the bank to withdraw the cash. I had to be at the Staples Center in three hours for the concert's 7:00 p.m. start time and faced at least a two-hour drive back to downtown L.A., longer if the traffic did not cooperate.

Also, I realized that I would have to find time to get to the hotel and give the Gibson a quick cleaning. It was quite grungy, like any guitar that had languished in its case for years. Still,

154

I considered myself especially fortunate to have received this rare bird and could not wait to see the look on Paul's face when I presented it.

This 1954 ES-350 Gibson was in all likelihood one of only a few of these guitars ever made in a left-handed configuration—a nearly unique instrument. Furthermore, it had remained completely unaltered, appearing virtually the same as it did in the fifty-year-old photo Georgia had sent me. In fact, it looked as if it had not been played much over the decades and was in excellent condition for its age. But my most pressing concern at the moment was whether I could drive my car back to Los Angeles quickly enough to bestow the guitar upon Sir Paul.

I did my best to get back in time, pushing eighty miles an hour when traffic allowed. And wouldn't you know it—as I put the pedal to the metal, I saw the ominous flashing red lights of a California Highway Patrol car in my rearview mirror. The one day that I could ill afford to be stopped. Help!

When the officer approached my car, I prompted him: "You're going to ask me why I was going so fast, right?" He responded coolly by asking for my license and registration. "You won't believe this, officer, but I'm rushing a guitar to Paul McCartney in Los Angeles."

"Sure you are. I've never heard that one before." He tipped up his dark glasses and peeked in the back seat and saw the old guitar case.

"That guitar?" he asked.

"Yes, Officer . . ." I stammered, searching for his name.

But it was only then that I looked at his shiny name badge, reading it out loud.

"Officer . . . Peppar?"

What I heard next was about to sum up the cosmic absurdity of the afternoon.

"Sergeant Peppar," he said, as he pointed to the stripes on his shirt.

Was this a mirage? Had I actually been stopped by Sgt. François Peppar of the California Highway Patrol on my way to a McCartney concert?

"No way . . ." I said, barely containing my laughter.

"Yaap," he said. "I've been getting laughed at for the past three years on that one."

The good sergeant walked back to his car, where I presumed he was going to retrieve his citation book.

Instead, when Sergeant Peppar returned, he didn't write me a ticket. But he sure did keep me on the side of the road reminiscing about Beatles songs for thirty minutes. "Slow down," he admonished before he sent me on my way with a smirk.

After arriving at my hotel, I quickly went to work cleaning and polishing the guitar, hoping to make it look somewhat presentable. The quick once-over did the trick. I laid the old Gibson back in its case, changed clothes, and sped across town to the show.

Pulling up, I could see that the arena was jam-packed, fans moving in long lines at every entrance. At the "will-call" window I was unceremoniously informed that they could not find my backstage passes. Precious minutes passed until finally the staff was able to locate them. But the obstacles did not stop there. At the VIP door I was greeted by a large security guard who pointed at the video device my cameraman had brought along to record the event—"You can't bring that in here" —and, nodding to the guitar case in my hand, he added, "and no, you can't do that."

I replied, "Mister, please, I'm here to see Paul McCartney and this guitar is for him. He's waiting on it, this very minute."

"Sorry," he said. "I've got strict orders. No cameras. And I'm sure they've got a regulation against musical instruments as well. I could lose my job."

It was then that I remembered the famous scene from *Beverly Hills Cop* where Eddie Murphy's character, Axel Foley, causes a ruckus by raising his voice in feigned outrage when he is denied entrance into a swank Rodeo Drive hotel. It was worth a try, I thought, and I did my thespian best.

"Look here," I said, getting right up in the guard's face, "I've come all the way down here from San Francisco and just drove clear to Palm Springs and back to pick up this guitar for Paul McCartney. It is probably the only one of its kind in the world. Do you want to tell Paul that he couldn't get his guitar because you were 'going by the book'?"

"The rules are the rules . . ." the guard tried to interject.

My voice was getting louder and my pitch edged higher as the words poured out faster.

"Well, these are going to be the last damn rules you'll ever have to worry about!" I snapped back, cranking up my tirade. "If you let me in immediately, you may still have a chance of keeping your job. If I don't get in, you will end up spending all day tomorrow looking in the 'help wanted' ads in the *L.A. Times*. And while you're at it, be sure to check out the front page. That's where you'll see the story of a security guard who was fired after he refused to let a guitar dealer give Paul McCartney a priceless, one-of-a-kind, left-handed guitar that he had been looking for all his life!"

The security guard looked hard at me. I looked back at him. He started laughing. I started laughing. "Are we cool?" I asked.

He might have been entertained by my acting debut, but he certainly didn't like it enough to let me through that door.

Frantic now, I rushed to another backstage door where a second guard proved more receptive. After describing my predicament, I beseeched him to go to the dressing rooms and try to make contact with Rusty Anderson.

"And who might that be?" he asked skeptically.

"He's Paul McCartney's guitar player and he knows all about this," was my exasperated reply.

"Well," the guard relented, "if he knows all about it, then I guess there won't be any problem now, will there?"

But again, it was not going to be so simple. I waited for another half hour only to discover that the guard had been unable to locate Rusty. At wits' end, I called upon everyone I could think of who might be able to help. It was no use. Without the go-ahead from someone with official status in Paul's entourage, I wasn't going to be joining the evening's entertainment.

By now the show was about to start. Tired and frustrated, I had no choice but to throw in the towel. I told the cameraman to go in and watch the show, then picked up the heavy guitar and camera and prepared to carry that weight all the way back to the parking lot, nearly a mile away. If I couldn't give the guitar to the person for whom it was intended, this was all just a bloody waste of time. I'm sure at that moment I looked and felt like a beaten man.

But as I started to walk away, I heard a faint voice behind me: "Hey, dude! Yo, Laurence Olivier . . . You with the guitar!" I turned to see the same security guard who had endured my Eddie Murphy improvisation, waving, rushing up to me.

"I'm sorry I doubted you, man," he said as he reached me, out of breath. "I got the word. It's all good. They're waiting. I'll get you there quick, it won't be long."

Like Lord Tennyson said of the charge of the light brigade, the day was saved.

This time around, I got the full-on VIP treatment. It was

nearly show time, but with three big men escorting me through the Staples Center, we parted the crowd like a husker going through a field of corn.

"I thought that you were trying to pull a fast one," the guard admitted to me as we approached the backstage area. "This stuff happens at every show."

As we finally approached the greenroom, Rusty burst into the hallway. "Where have you been?" he asked. "The show is about to start."

I started to explain my whole ordeal, but he cut me short. "No time, man," he exclaimed, looking at his watch. "We're about to go on. Let me see if I can get Paul." He hurried away and returned a few minutes later, motioning me to follow him. "Come on," he urged. "We only have a minute."

I followed him down yet another long hall until we stopped outside of Paul's dressing room.

"He's coming right out," Rusty reassured me.

My cameraman Jack and I joined the gaggle of people outside the dressing room. Jack brought my video camera, ready for a good vantage on the upcoming proceedings, when another guard told us we could not take videos. Rusty stepped in, relieving my fears that the moment would come and go without being chronicled. The group's official photographers and videographers would take the pictures, he explained.

Band members began emerging from dressing rooms, a few even remembering us from our last encounter in Sacramento.

Then Paul himself appeared. "Hello, people," he said affably. He looked around, smiling at everyone in the hallway, and then, for some reason, focused on the ornate fountain pen with its musical note clip that my cameraman prominently displayed in his breast pocket. Sir Paul, with a mischievous glint in his eye, went right up and plucked the pen out of his pocket, eliciting a mortified look—until Paul reached into his own jacket pocket and pulled out an identical pen.

"Mine's from Tiffany," he said with a laugh.

After what seemed like an eternity, Rusty cleared his throat and said, "Paul, this is Michael."

"Well, hello, Michael. To what do I owe the extreme pleasure of this surprising visit?"

"Ahh, hello. Ahh, I have a . . . ahh . . ."

"Michael's got a guitar he wants to show you." Rusty interjected.

"Oh, right. Right. I've been looking forward to it. Yes." Paul replied.

Yet I could tell from the guarded look in his eye that Paul assumed I was going to simply show him an expensive instrument and then attempt to foist it on him at an inflated price. "What is it?"

"It's one of those funny guitars that only look normal when you hold it up in front of a mirror," I said, trying to defuse the tension, but all I got back was a blank look. So I opened the case and pulled out the vintage lefty.

I could see delight in Paul's eyes when he finally gazed upon that 1954 Gibson. Instantly, every hassle and inconvenience I had endured was worth the effort.

"Oh, this is quite nice, yes, quite nice indeed." he said, taking the guitar I handed to him. "Let's just have a look." Sir Paul looked the guitar over very closely, and as he did he apparently mumbled some obscure *Mersey Beat* reference that I didn't quite understand—but I could feel that it was a positive sentiment. Finally he asked, "What year was it made?" I told him all the details, including the fact that it was possibly the only left-handed model ever made of this particular instrument still left in existence. Paul was obviously excited.

"I was twelve years old when that was built," he said, clearly moved by the rich history of this vintage instrument. After a few minutes of careful inspection he looked up and said: "Shall we get down to it?" I could see that he was bracing himself for a hefty price tag.

"What are your plans for her?"

"I'm going to give it to you," I replied, "that is, if you want it."

Paul's skepticism melted into a look of sheer joy and I was reminded once again of how much of his exuberant personality is tied up in the music he shares with the world. He lit up like a slot machine.

"If I want it?" he echoed, wrapping his arm around the guitar. "Blimey! You aren't getting this one back, mate. It's absolutely brilliant." He looked around to share his pleasure with the others gathered in the hall—now a not-so-small crowd that included actor Alec Baldwin, who had been attracted to the unfolding scene. There were murmurs of approval and Paul pointed to the photographers, instructing them to capture the moment; two videographers and several still photographers started shooting away.

I felt a warm glow as the flashbulbs and excitement lit the room around us. I knew my gift had really touched Paul and that I had picked exactly the right instrument. Paul put his arm around me as the scene was filmed. Now the crowd grew and many camera clicks and flashes went off. For that one brief, shining moment I thought, "So this is what it's like to be a Beatle!" Then, as quickly as it had begun, it was time for the show to start and the band began walking toward the stage. But Paul was not quite ready to leave.

"I want to hear this guitar," he said, looking around for his stage manager. "Let's put some new strings on this thing."

The stage manager, who was responsible for every aspect of

the concert, appeared by his side. "We don't have time for that Paul, not now . . ." he said, hinting that it was show time. "You're meant to be on stage in just a few minutes."

"Tonight, Paul," I interjected, "you're a working stiff."

"Right you are, man," he replied, "I'm off to work." He turned and followed the stage manager for about thirty feet, but then stopped—ran back to the guitar, grabbed it, and carried it into his dressing room. He twisted the door handle to make doubly certain it was locked. "This doesn't happen every day ya' know . . . Somebody walks up and gives you a guitar that you've always wanted."

I replied, "Something tells me it happens to you a lot more often than it does to me." Paul just laughed, thanked me again, and bade me adieu. A few moments later he was taking a bow before the ecstatic, sold-out crowd.

That evening will always stand as one of the most memorable in my life. I had the chance to meet an icon, a man whom I consider to be one of humanity's best friends, and to give him something that I think he really appreciated. It was a moment that gave fresh meaning to my love of music, musicians, and musical instruments. It was really something.

The End.

Epilogue

M usic is a fabulous gift. It carries great feelings, associa-
tions, and memories. It is a cliché, but in a very real way,
music has been the soundtrack to our lives—at least in our generation. Music is the way we express our common connection,
our shared humanity through an artistic language. And when I
contemplate all the pleasure music has brought to my life and
the lives of others, I know I made the correct career choice.

But when I look at the latest generation of guitar players,
I see few today who have the talent of those I grew up with:
performers such as Johnny Winter, Rory Gallagher, Ronnie
Montrose, Stevie Ray Vaughan, Carlos Santana, Neal Schon,
Eric Clapton, Jimmy Page, Keith Richards, Ron Wood, John
McLaughlin, Robin Trower, Jeff Beck, Joe Satriani, Billy Gib-
bons, Peter Frampton, Jimi Hendrix, and so on. These are all
bona fide guitar virtuosos and artists. Where are the young gui-
tar geniuses today: John Mayer, Kenny Wayne Shepherd, Joe
Bonamassa, Jack White . . . is that it?

The irony is that while there are more people playing guitar than ever, only a few young players are considered guitar
legends. Why? I think we have entered an era where the forces

that existed after World War II—forces that produced that amazing crop of musicians—have dissipated. Those trends included a great new wave of freedom and euphoria after the end of the worldwide conflagration. In Britain, for example, money was exceedingly scarce in the post–World War II world. Many of the great emerging guitarists had very little money to spend on entertainment and leisure, allowing them more time to focus on playing their instruments. This also provided them the time to join a band—and to practice and play music together.

Also consider that from 1945 to 1960 kids did not have the variety in entertainment that our youth have today. In 1960, there were only a few channels of television, AM and FM radio, record players, books, and magazines. Today's landscape is dramatically different. Kids have access to all of that media, plus thousands of channels of cable or satellite television, as well as the Internet with millions of websites—including social media, tweeting, blogging, dating, auction, travel, YouTube . . . it goes on forever. And there are thousands of video games, including formerly popular music games like Guitar Hero and Rock Band. In short, today music competes with a vast array of other media and activities. And so music is much less a focus than it was in the baby boomer generation.

The great wave of technological advance has played a role in the demise of the importance of music. Think of great albums made in music's heyday. Take Fleetwood Mac's album *Rumours*—produced over the course of a year—with all band members sequestered at the Record Plant recording studio in Sausalito, California. They collaborated under the painful stress of turbulent interpersonal relations. Today such forced collaboration wouldn't happen. Artists would work at home recording studios, miles or even continents apart. Some say that such separation can hurt the music; it isn't just mastering the material that creates inspiration—it's the interaction and on-the-spot chemistry of the artists.

At the same time, file-sharing and digital-downloading technologies have eviscerated the profitability of the major record labels. Top record labels today simply do not sign and develop pop bands over a long period of time as they did in the past. Now an MBA is often running the show at the label, not the music industry A&R veterans who nurtured talented bands into greatness. End result: today we get Britney Spears instead of Bruce Springsteen; *American Idol* instead of Ahmet Ertegün.

As such, we may be in for a continued and prolonged period of musical mediocrity. Surprisingly, this could be good for the vintage guitar market. For years to come people will be nostalgic for the great music era from 1950 to 1975. And it is likely they will have similar sentiment for the musical instruments of that era, especially the symbol of that era: the guitar.

The other side of the equation is the possibility that the vintage guitar collecting "boom" may have been just a short-term phenomenon. I remember calling esteemed vintage guitar dealer George Gruhn in 1977 to ask him his thoughts about the future of vintage guitar collecting. Mr. Gruhn doled out some prophetic advice: "It's all tied to the continued popularity of rock music, or other guitar-based music." Since the day I made that telephone call in 1977, the value of my 1955 Fender Stratocaster soared from $500 to a peak of $50,000 in 2007—the starting price multiplied by a hundred. After the "Great Recession" in 2008, the price of that same guitar dropped in half to about $25,000, but now in 2015 prices seem to be rebounding.

The real question is: where do we go from here? My observation is that unless the current generation of twenty-five- to thirty-five-year-olds begins to seriously pick up the guitar-collecting baton, the vintage guitar market as a whole may have already peaked. Just like any maturing market, you need new buyers to replace the collectors who are leaving the market. And I have not seen guitar players from those younger demographics becoming avid collectors as yet. One of the many reasons is this: today's guitar heroes do not play vintage guitars at live concerts like they did in the old days. And who can blame them?

Take for instance Kirk Hammett from Metallica. Kirk is known to have an expansive vintage guitar collection. But we do not see Kirk playing a 1959 Les Paul on stage. For the most part he performs with a new guitar that he receives an endorsement to play live. Fair enough; like I said, everyone is entitled to make a profit. But when Kirk and I were growing up (we went to the same high school), a 1963 Stratocaster would have cost $300. That was about the price of a new Stratocaster at the time. It was not so valuable that you would be afraid to bring it on stage. However, since that same Strat would now be worth $15,000, it becomes much less likely for a player to take that guitar out on the road to gig with it.

Imagine the concern that a player gigging with a '59 Les Paul or a '58 Explorer on stage would feel. Dropping the guitar and breaking the headstock on a guitar like that could profoundly diminish the value; hence, few play these treasures on stage anymore. This in turn has actually hurt the visibility of true vintage instruments. When I was a youngster, I recall seeing the English band Wishbone Ash playing live with a 1958 Flying V, a 1959 Les Paul Sunburst, and a 1956 Stratocaster. Not only did they sound spectacular, the instruments gave the band a major mojo. When I saw Robin Trower perform in San Francisco in 1977, he had a phalanx of mid-sixties custom color Stratocasters on stage as back-ups: Candy Apple Red, Lake Placid Blue, Shoreline Gold, Sonic Blue, etc. That was the best advertising for vintage guitars that money could buy. And while a few rock stars still play vintage guitars on stage, few seem to bring the heavy artillery like one would see in the old days; the rare Les Pauls, Teles, Strats, Flying V's, and Explorers seem to stay home in the vault.

Another factor is that legacy guitar manufacturers are now making excellent "vintage reissue" instruments that are a fraction of the price of their vintage counterparts. Back in the 1970s, a vintage 1959 Les Paul Sunburst could be had for roughly $2,500; a new Les Paul Custom retailed for $1,000 at that time. This was not a huge differential in price, but the vintage Les Paul was a vastly superior instrument. Today that same 1959 Les Paul is worth over $200,000, and the new reissue costs $4,000 and is a virtual copy of the original. These new Gibson reissues are much better in my opinion than the standard 1970s Gibson guitars. The bottom line is that today you can purchase an excellent copy of the vintage original for a fraction of the price. These reissues have put severe pressure on the vintage guitar market. These facts beg the question: what is in store for the future of this market?

Well, Mr. Gruhn had it right back in 1977. The vintage market is tied to the continued popularity of the music that the guitar has become associated with. Anglo-American pop music will likely be with us for the foreseeable future. If this is true, vintage guitars will most likely remain popular. No question, the American-made instruments are popular around the world. On the other hand, the primary expansion and popularity of American-made vintage guitars may have already peaked. I suspect that the high end of the vintage market will continue to hold up. After all, it only takes two wealthy buyers competing for expensive vintage guitars to make a market. This was the case when Scott Chinery and Tadeo Tsumura were competing for the best arch-top jazz guitars back in the 1990s. Once these gentlemen left the market, the prices of arch-tops first stagnated, then declined.

Since wealthy people by definition will usually have disposable income and will want the best that money can buy, D-45 Martin guitars from the 1930s, Gibson Les Paul Standard Sunburst guitars from the late 1950s, and 1950s Fender Stratocaster guitars will always be sought after. But what about the middle of the market and the low end? I think this is the more difficult question, and its answer is much more tied to musical trends than other social factors. We shall see what we shall see.

For the Guitar Men and Women of the future, I have some further thoughts. There is a good living to be made on the road in search of rare and valuable vintage guitars, but you have to develop patience and interpersonal skills. You must love talking to people and listening to their stories. Willingness to travel is also indispensable; I have driven over a million miles in search of stringed treasures. You also need a lot of energy. This life can really take it out of you and is definitely not for those with a slow metabolism or a short attention span. And it can be very lonely out there, take my word. If you have a hard time keeping yourself company, this occupation is not for you. If you are married, make sure your spouse agrees to you being away for long periods. If you're single, one hazard of this job is the complete lack of a domestic or social life.

The Guitar Men and Women of tomorrow must have the skills of a door-to-door salesman, the stamina of a truck driver, the inclinations of a celibate, and the energy of a triathlete. And of course, they need to learn the difference between a fake 1959 Les Paul and the real McCoy.

Buying and selling guitars? It ain't for everybody. But I would not trade a moment of my life. Well, maybe for that 1958 Gibson Moderne . . .

Acknowledgments

This book is dedicated to my grandparents and to my mother and father.

Thanks to my extended family. And thanks to my mentors Jack and Marge Ruggles and Bill and Joyce Mori; also thanks to Robin Williams; Charylu Roberts; William Seidlitz; Kermit Goodman; Rick McCarthy; Serge Wilson; Kit Knudsen; Robin Lee; Charles Flynn; Ronnie and Leighsa Montrose; Rusty Anderson; Ron Garcia; Jeff Burkhart; Terri Beausejour; fellow guitar dealers Norman Harris, Jay Rosen, Larry Wexer, David Swartz, and Andrew Berlin; Dave Belzer; the Scott Chinery family, and Perry Margouleff. Also thanks to my professors Arthur Quinn, John Dolan, Bridget Connelly, R. T. B. Langhorne, Sir Harry Hinsley, and P. J. Allott. And thanks to all the friends who kindly read the early and late drafts of this book with invaluable comments; and to the hundreds and hundreds of families who invited me into their homes to allow me the privilege of hearing their stories and buying their treasured musical instruments. I also wish to give special thanks to the folks at Hal Leonard: John Cerullo, Jessica Burr, and especially the copyeditor Zahra Brown. Thank you all for making this book possible!

Index